AF522591

NEW DIMENSIONS IN HUMAN RESOURCE MANAGEMENT

NEW DIMENSIONS IN HUMAN RESOURCE MANAGEMENT

By

Dr. Shoeb Ahmad

Associate Professor
Deptt. of Management
Bahir Dar University
Ethiopia

DISCOVERY PUBLISHING HOUSE PVT. LTD.

NEW DELHI-110 002

Published by:
Tilak Wasan
DISCOVERY PUBLISHING HOUSE PVT. LTD.
4831/24, Prahlad Street, Ansari Road
Darya Ganj, New Delhi-110002 (India)
Phone: +91-11-23279245, 43764432
Fax: +91-11-23253475
E-mail: parul.wasan@gmail.com
info@discoverypublishinggroup.com
web: www.discoverypublishinggroup.com

First Edition: **2011**
ISBN: 978-81-8356-803-6

New Dimensions in Human Resource Management

Printed at:
Shree Balaji Art Press
Delhi

Dedicated

to

My Parents

Preface

In order to provide further assistance to readers a glossary of useful terms have been included in the area of human resource management and to provide a consolidated reading list of key texts in the subject. It has a broad view of human resource management which also has its strategic and operational implications. It is structured in group of related chapters each having a separate theme according to the common core syllabus for all management students. The initial chapters of this book are devoted to the discussion of human resource management and problems of underdeveloped countries like India. Then turn to a discussion on job analysis, methods for manpower search and recruitment processes.

The stage is, thus, set for a discussion of issue specifically related to manpower training and development and career management. This book also examines performance appraisal and compensation management. The most attractive part of this book is in respect of employee relation and collective bargaining, grievance handling and disciplinary action.

Thus, the utility of the book is enhanced by the fact that it is the book which deals satisfactorily with latest topics prescribed for the studies of human resource management. The treatment is exhaustive and analytical in nature. The cases have been appended at the end of the book that probes deep into the subject and furnishes valuable information which is enlightening. A list of questions has also been added at the end of each chapter for the guidance of students, on account of these reasons.

The book is ideal for students who have taken up a basic course of human resources and management and wish to specialize in the area of human resource management. It aims at those pursuing management courses for a variety of Business Studies Degrees.

I am also thankful to my publisher Discovery Publishing House Pvt. Ltd., New Delhi for publishing the book timely. Suggestions from the reader are most welcome to make the book useful for the students.

Dr. Shoeb Ahmad

Acknowledgement

First of all I express my heartiest gratitude to the Almighty for his mercy due to which this project could be possible on my part to prepare and present it.

I express my deepest and sincere gratitude and unbounded indeptedness to all the people who have been patiently supportive, encouraging and helpful throughout completion of this project.

I express my sincere and unbounded gratitude to my family members specially my father- Prof. Zeyauddin Ahmad (Ex V.C), mother- Ishrat Ahmad, inlaws-Mrs. and Mr. S. M. Siddiqui and other family supporters who have rendered unconditional support, inspiration and encouragement in this endeavour.

I am thankful to everyone in my circle of educationists for getting inspiration to write such a book covering the latest syllabus of 'Human Resource Management'. I am grateful to my wife for their support, guidance and inspiration for writing this book covering emerging topics in the area of human resources.

My special thanks goes to leadership of Bahir Dar university, Ethiopia: Awoke Berihum, Fyory and all my faculty colleagues particularly my management group for creating a stimulating and supportive work environment.

I am also thankful to my publisher and other members from Discovery Publishing House, New Delhi, who have shown keen interest and published the book timely. Suggestions from the reader are most welcome to make the book useful for the students.

Dr. Shoeb Ahmad

Contents

CHAPTER 1 Introduction to Human Resource Management

CONCEPT

Human resource is one of the most valuable and unique assets of an organisation. It is one of the most complex and challenging fields of modern management. A human resource manager has to build-up an effective workforce, handle the expectations of the employees and ensure that they perform at their best.

Successful management of an organisation's human resources is an exciting, dynamic and challenging field, especially at a time when companies are globalising larger numbers of knowledge workers.

Anything living or dead in use for some specific purpose/ reason, may be seen as a resource depending upon its use, objective and characteristics. The total skill, knowledge, ideas and experiences of human beings specific to personnel attached to an organisation for which they are suitably rewarded is HR and the management of the same is HRM.

It is concerned with human problems of an organisation so that individuals can contribute maximum for accomplishment of common goals and at the same time attain social satisfaction. It is the process of binding people and the organisation together so that objectives of each are accomplished.

Success of an organisation depends upon the quality of HR. Hence, acquiring and retaining good human resources is a precondition for any organisation to be effective and efficient.

The HRM is a process with four functions – acquiring, developing, motivating and retaining human resources. Acquisition starts with planning and ends with staffing. The development function has three dimensions – employees training, management development, and career development. The motivation function identifies the motivational needs of employees and also the ways to inspire them. The retention function provides a conducive work environment to the employees and nurtures them to make them feel committed and attached to the organisation.

These four functions and their constituent sub-functions have changed over the years due to changes in the social and political environment of business and as a result of new development in the management thought.

"Personnel function is concerned with the procurement, development, compensation, integration, and maintenance of the personnel of an organisation towards accomplishment of the organisation's major goals and policies".

—E. P. Flippo

"Human Resource management is that part of management function which is primarily concerned with human relationships in an organisation. Its objective is the maintenance of those relationships which enable all those engaged in the undertaking to make their maximum contribution for effective working of that undertaking."

—Indian Institute of Personnel Management, Calcutta

"Human Resource Management is the art of acquiring, developing and maintaining a competent workforce in such a manner as to accomplish with maximum efficiency and economy the functions and objectives of the organisation." —***Society for personnel Administration of America***

"Human Resource Management is that aspect of management having as its goal the effective utilization of the labor resources of an organisation".

—***Paul. G. Hastings***

Perspectives

The present chapter of the book deals with different pertinent questions. What is human resource management (?), what should be its constituent activities (?), what is their importance (?), how do they help to achieve the organizational purpose (?) what is their relationship with other organizational activities (?), where do they fit (?), etc.

The answers to above have to be found in order to understand the appropriate place and role of human resource management in the structure and activities of the organisation.

After examining various definitions of human resource management given above, we come across the following major characteristics :

- It is concerned with employees both as individuals as well as groups engaged in attaining organisational goals.
- It is concerned with the development of human resources to the maximum possible extent so that they may be able to derive greatest possible satisfaction from their jobs.
- It covers all levels and all categories of employees in an organisation.
- It focuses to attain the goals of an organisation and willing co-operation of people.
- It is not the sole responsibility of personnel manager but embraces all line managers and staff managers in an organisation.

Thus, human resource management is concerned with procurement and maintenance of capable and effective workforce in such a manner that the employees and the groups feel a sense of involvement and commitment to the organisation.

We can deal with the above discussion in the following mathematical model:

Step I – IR (industrial resources)

Step II – MA (managerial action)

Step III – Re (results)

According to Step I – Step II – Step III

For better manager, R – M – R = Me

Where R – M – R is resource managerial result and Me = managerial efficiency.

Since, Mi = index of managerial efficiency

So, Mi = Me

Also,

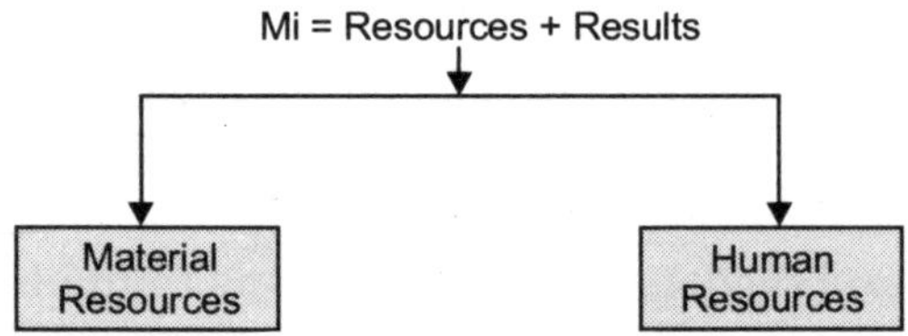

Material resources ⇌ Human Resources, Thus, in diagrammetrical representation

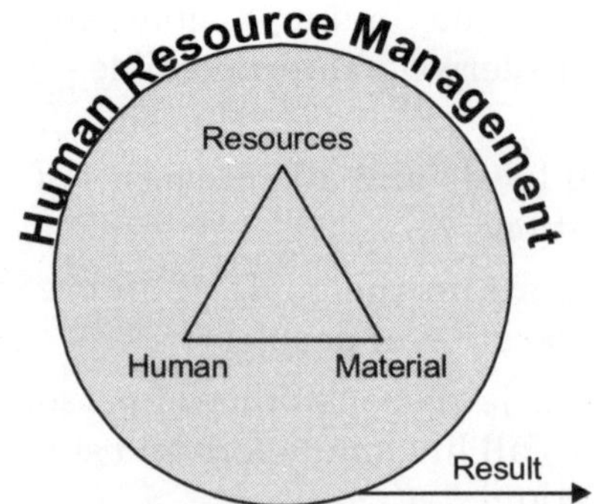

Since, the above functions are common to all managers including human resource manager and management involves accomplishing results through people, it is rightly said that management is human resource management.

History of Human Resource Management

There is a vast difference between HRM and the personnel management. During 1990s a great change in the nature and scope of personnel management was observed. Functions of personnel management not only involve labour welfare, industrial relations and physical administration but also developing relationship with the employees on long term basis and treating employees as a part of the organisation. Hence, the American Society for Personnel Administration supported to change its name to as Human Resource Management. Over the past eighty years, the scientific management approach and the human relations approach appeared and then disappeared too. But of late, human resource approach has acquired prominence.

Scientific Management Approach

In 1911, F.W. Taylor wrote the principles of scientific management so he was considered "Father of Scientific Management". In 1878, he began to experiment an engineer and inventor with new managerial concepts while being employed at the Midvale Steel Co. At. Midvale, his rise from labourer to Chief Engineer within six years of period gave him the opportunity to tackle work shirking problem. According to him, employees deliberately worked slower than their capabilities. He advocated the solution of right people for right jobs, training them adequately, placing them in jobs according to their suitability and remunerating them handsomely.

Taylor considered that through time and motion study it is possible to fix a standard time for doing a particular task. To encourage workers to complete the work within the standard time, he recommended two price rates. If a man performs the work within or less than the standard time he should be paid a higher price rate. If he does not complete the work within the standard time, he should be given a lower price rate. For example, if the standard production has been fixed for 8 units/day for 8 hours, the higher price rate for 8 units or more may be Rs. 8 per unit while the lower price rate to less than 8 units may be 80/unit.

The scientific management approach resulted in work methods and techniques that emphasised employees output.

Personnel departments of big manufacturing organisations have been responsible for recruiting, selecting and training staff and ensuring their health and safety. Also, personnel departments of many big companies supported welfare programmes such as job training, company housing, employees loans, insurance plans and recreational programs. However, such practices were not very successful in bringing about *behavioural changes* and *productivity gains* desired by the management. That is why the employee welfare programmes became less popular during 1920s and 1930s. hence, the personal departments of big organisations were interested to implement scientific management techniques.

Human Relations Approach

The Hawthorne studies conducted during 1930s and 1940s, forced the organisations to shift attention from scientific management approach to human relations approach. The results of these studies suggested that employees productivity was affected not only by the way the job was designed for the economic rewards but also by certain social and psychological factors. Although the human relations approach was instrumental in improving the work environment for many workers, it was not very successful in improving their productivity and job satisfaction due to many reasons. During the 1950s and 1960s, the human relations approach began to be seen as outdated, and was abandoned by many organisations.

Human Resources Approach

In 1970s, research in behavioral sciences suggested not to treat people as factors of production only but also as resources or human beings who act on the basis of emotions alone. The human resources approach is based on principles like ;

- Employees are assets to an organisation.
- Policies, programs and practices must help employees in their work and personal development.
- It is necessary to create and maintain environment conducive to work.

Functions of Human Resource Management

Every manager gets the things done through people. Individual goals and aspirations should be in alignment with organisational goals for the successful handling of a business. Managing people is one of the biggest challenges for any manager because

- Individuals differ from each other in terms of their values, attitudes, beliefs and culture.
- Stimulating and motivational factors differ from individual to individual. It is important to understand the individual needs of these employees.
- The expectations of employees of today are much greater when compared to the employees of yesterdays.

A manager must understand and accept the fact that individuals create excellence not the organisations.

The HRM functions can be broadly classified into two categories:

1. Managerial functions, and
2. Operative functions.

Managerial Functions

Managerial functions of the human resource department are planning, organising, directing, staffing and controlling.

Planning

Planning is the primary functions of management as without it nothing can be performed. It helps to decide in advance the personnel programs and the changes required for the achievement of organisational goals. It also helps to identify human resource requirements and forecasting individual personnel needs and planning for selection and training procedures, etc.

Organizing

It is the distribution of work in groups or sections for effective performance. Also, it indicates the position of each person in the organisation and finds out the path through which the communication should flow.

Staffing

It is the process of obtaining and maintaining capable and competent personnel in various positions at all levels. It encompasses manpower planning, recruitment, selection, placement, induction and orientation, transfer, career progression and separation.

Directing

It is the process of making the workers learn techniques to perform the assigned jobs. It ensures maximum employees contribution and also helps in establishing sound industrial and human relations. It coordinates between different departments to ensure maximum utilization of all the resources including human resources.

Controlling

This function measures performance against goals and plans, identifies deviations and by placing the process back on track, helps in the accomplishment of plans.

Operative Functions

The operative functions of HRM are related to specific activities of HRM, viz. employment, development, compensation, and employee relations. The HR function is unique to every organisation and the activities of the HR department differ from one organisation to the other.

The various operative functions of HRM are discussed below:

Employment

Employment is the first operative function of HRM. This involves procuring and employing individuals who have suitable knowledge, skills, experience and aptitude necessary to perform various jobs. It includes functions such as job analysis, human resource planning, recruitment, selection, placement, and induction.

Job Analysis

It is the process by which the tasks which comprise the job are determined and the skills and abilities required to perform it successfully are identified. It involves:

- Preparing job description, job specification, job requirements and employee specification so that the HR manager could determine the nature, levels and quantum of human resources required.
- Providing the guides, plans, and the basis for job design and redesign.

Human Resource Planning

It involves forecasting for the human resource requirement of an organisation and the future supply of human resources, and making suitable adjustments between these two in correlation with organisational plan. It also involves assessing the possibility of developing the human resources to match the requirements by introducing appropriate changes in the functions of HRM. It involves:

- Estimating the present and future manpower requirements on the basis of long range plans and organisational objectives.

- Estimating the net human resource requirements on the basis of the present inventor of human resources.
- Taking measures to mould, change and develop the existing employees.
- Developing action plans to attract and acquire valuable human resources.

Recruitment

It is the process of seeking and attracting prospective candidates against a vacancy in an organisation. It involves:

- Extracting new sources of applicants and also developing the new sources.
- Identifying or creating new sources of recruitment.
- Stimulating and attracting the candidates to apply for jobs in the organisation.
- Deciding the recruitment procedure.

Selection

It is the process of identifying and establishing the credentials of a candidate for a job to ensure success. This function deals with

- Scanning the application forms.
- Identifying and developing suitable and reliable testing techniques.
- Involving the candidates and fixing their salaries and benefits.
- Formulating medical fitness policy and examination.
- Intimating the candidates including the ones who are not selected, about the results of the selection process.
- Employing the selected candidates.

Placement

Once, a selected candidate accepts the offer of employment given by an organisation, his placement has to be decided based on the needs of the organisation.

Induction

Introducing a new employee to the organisation, its business, culture, values and beliefs, and practices and procedures is termed as induction. It also includes helping the employee to be acquainted with his new job and his tasks and responsibilities.

Human Resource Development

Human Resource Development (HRD) is the process of training and developing the employees to improve and update their knowledge and skills also attitudes, beliefs and values to match the organisational requirements / needs. It is a continuous process that takes into consideration both the present and future organisational requirements. It includes performance appraisal, training, management development and career planning and development.

Performance Appraisal

It is the process of evaluating the performance of an employee on the job and developing a plan for improvement. This includes an assessment of the strengths and weaknesses of an employee and drawing up a development plan in consultation with him to prepare him for future tasks and responsibilities in the organisation. Performance Appraisal includes.

- Designing a performance appraisal system that suits the organisational needs and culture.
- Developing suitable methods.
- Training the employees in conducting appraisals.
- Implementing the system effectively
- Obtaining feedback on its effectiveness and making necessary changes timely.

Training

It is the systematic development of the knowledge, skills and attitudes required to perform a given task or job successfully in an individual. It includes:

- Identifying the training needs of the individuals.
- Designing suitable training programs to eliminate the gaps in knowledge, skill or attitude.
- Conducting training programs.
- Evaluating the effectiveness of the training programs and making necessary changes.

Management Development

It is the concept of developing the employees of an organisation to meet future changes and challenges. It includes forecasting the human resource demands of an organisation and gearing up to meet these demands.

Career Planning

It refers to identify one's career goals and formulating plans of reaching them through various means like education, work experience, etc. Career development looks at individuals' goals from the point of view of the organisation, where as career planning looks at the same from the individual's view point.

Compensation

It includes all the extrinsic rewards that an employee receives during and after the course of his job for his contribution to the organisation. Compensation encompasses base salary, incentivs, bonus and benefits and is based on job evaluation.

Job Evaluation

It is a systematic determination of the value of each job in relation to other jobs in the organisation, industry, and in the market. It involves

- Identifying/designing suitable job evaluation.
- Evaluating various jobs.

Ascertaining relative wages. The process of formulating and operating a suitable wage and salary program is known as wag and salary administration. It includes

- Conducting wage and salary survey in the market and in the industry;
- Determining wage and salary rates on the basis of various factors such as law, equity, fairness and performance.
- Implementing wage and salary administration programs.
- Evaluating the effectiveness of these programmes.

Incentives : These are the rewards an employee earns in addition to his or her regular wages.

Bonus : It is primarily a share in the surplus or bounty and is directly related to the organisation's performance. In India, the payment of bonus is a very popular means of rewarding employees and is governed by the Payment of Bonus Act 1965.

Fringe benefits : These are those monetary and non-monetary benefits given to employees during their employment and sometimes, also in the post employment period. These benefits provide a sense of security to the employee and keep them committed to the organisation. Some of the fringe benefits include:

- Disablement benefits
- Housing facilities
- Canteen facilities
- Conveyance facilities
- Educational facilities for employees and their children
- Credit facilities
- Recreational facilities
- Medical and welfare facilities
- Post-retirement benefits
- Company stores
- Legal aid.

Employee Relations

Employee relations deal with the employees in the organisational context, as a social group that contributes to the organisation. It includes:

- Increasing employees productivity
- Keeping the employees satisfied and motivated
- Developing team building team management and leadership skills in employees.
- Designing and implementing a fast and suitable grievance management system
- Ensuring discipline among the employees by prompt action.
- Supporting employees through counseling.
- Enhancing the quality of work and personal life of employees

An average employee desires his manager to possess the following characteristics:

- Be genuinely interested in the employee
- Identify the strengths and suggestions for improvement.
- Identify the weaknesses
- Take a personal interest in the employee
- Be willing to listen and accept
- Reward the employee for his contribution.
- Have faith and confidence in employees' abilities.
- Be frank and open in his dealings with the employee as well as the organisation.

HRM Model

In the recent decade, HR faces various challenges in order to motivate employees to work as a team for achieving maximum customer satisfaction.

Environmental Challenges

These are external force affecting the enterprise and are beyond the control of management. Some of these are identified as increase in the competition. They may be on account of entry of multinational, lower import duties, collaborators becoming competitors and providing multiple service.

The American Society for Training and Development (ASTD) has stressed on the following to meet these challenges efficiently.

Training and Development

Employee training is a specialized and one of the fundamental operative functions of HR management. It is the systematic development of knowledge, skills and attitude required to perform a given task or job successfully. It includes:

- Identifying the training needs of the individuals.
- Designing suitable training program to eliminate the gaps in knowledge, skill or attitude.
- Conducting the training program.
- Evaluating the training programs and making necessary changes.

These programmes fill the gap between

- What someone can do
- What someone would be able to do

Development

- It provides people to do better in their existing job and prepares them for higher future responsibilities.
- It builds on strengths and helps to overcome the weaknesses and also ensures that the organisation has the expertise it needs to achieve the strategic objective.

Organisation Development

According to Dale S. Beach, organisation development is "a complex educational strategy designed to increase organisational effectiveness and wealth through planned intervention by a consultant using theory and techniques of applied behavioral science". Organisation Development (OD) concentrates on people's dimensions like norms, values, attitudes, relationships and organisational climate. The OD efforts broadly aim at improving the organisational effectiveness and job satisfaction of employees.

Organisation / Job Design

Organisation design deals with structural aspects of organisations. It aims at analysis roles and relationships so that collective effort could be explicitly organized to achieve specific ends. It is the process of determining the specific task and responsibilities to be carried out by each member of the organisation. It has many implications for HR management both in the content and one's job. Ability to influence contents and level of performance affect a person's motivation and job satisfaction.

Planning

It helps in finding out/determining in advance the personal programs and the chances required for the achievement of organisational goals. It also helps in identifying human resource requirement and forecasting individual personal needs and planning for selection and training procedure, etc.

Selection and Staffing

The selection process involves judging the candidates on a variety of dimensions ranging from the concrete and measurable like years of experience to the abstract and personal like leadership potential.

While it is important to have a good organisation structure, it is more important to fill the job with right people. Staffing includes several sub-functions:

(*i*) Recruitment or getting applications for the job as they open up.

(*ii*) Selection of the best qualified from those who seek the jobs.

(*iii*) Transfers and promotions

(*iv*) Training those who need further instruction to perform their work effectively or to qualify for promotions.

Importance and Need for Proper Staffing: There are a number of advantages of proper and efficient staffing:

(*i*) It helps in discovering talented and competent workers and developing them to move up the corporate ladder.

(*ii*) It ensures greater production by putting the right man in the right job.

(*iii*) It helps to avoid a sudden disruption of an enterprise's production run by indicating shortages of personnel if any, in advance.

(*iv*) It helps to prevent under-utilization of personnel and the resultant high labor cost and low profit margins.

(*v*) It provides information to management for internal succession of managerial personnel in the event of an unanticipated turnover.

Personnel Research and Information Systems

The term 'research' means a systematic and goal-oriented investigation of facts that seeks to establish a relationship between two or more phenomena. It can lead to understanding and improvement in HRM practices.

Compensation/Benefits

Wages and salaries –The payment is aimed at reimbursing employees for their work and motivating them to perform to the best of their abilities. In addition to pay, most employees receive benefits such as ESI, leave travel concession, and non-financial rewards such as security, recognition and privileges.

Determining wage and salary payments is one of the most critical aspects of HRM because

(*i*) The organisations rewards system has a profound effect on the recruitment, satisfaction and motivation of employees and

(*ii*) Wage and salaries represent a considerable cost to the employer.

Employee Assistance

Employee assistance focuses on providing personal problem solving and counselling to individual employees.

Union/Labour Relations

Unions are born because employees are frustrated and fail to achieve certain goals. Unionism is only a countervailing technique available to achieve these goals. The establishment of labour relations depends on constructive attitude of both the management and the union.

The challenges also include market characteristics. Some of them as changes in economy, decline of traditional manufacturing industries, huge underutilised capital (industries), restrictive, legislation, rapid changes in technologies and dumping tendency of developed nations etc.

Organisational Challenges

Every enterprise faces the following organisational challenges. Some are :

(*i*) stiff demand customers cost, quality, delivery schedule, service etc.

(*ii*) impediments in acquiring latest technology.

(*iii*) resource crunch

(*iv*) decreasing influence of trade unions

(*v*) structure creating delays in organisational restructure

(*vi*) demand for decentralization

(*vii*) low utilization of resources

(*viii*) rise of individualism

(*ix*) aging workforce

(*x*) organisational culture, norms, values and

(*xi*) old technology vs new technology and related problems.

Human Resource Challenges

Human resource challenges are matching of individual and organisation needs, rapid erosion in value and ethics, demand for result orientation rather than activity orientation, demand for more empowerment by employees, losing talent due to luring by competitors, increased job insecurity, and the demand for the best pay package. These challenges subject to HRM condition of creating new environment for new period.

ROLE OF HR EXECUTIVES

HRM is a part of every manager's job. It has to be noted that in a dynamic working environment, boundaries and specific dimensions of any role cannot be clearly defined. The specific role of the HR manager has taken many styles like.

The Executive

An HR specialists carry out certain HR activities like recruitment, redeployment and compensation, etc. He can also interpret the complex labor laws and legislations that are applicable in day-to-day work.

The Facilitator

Organisational activities require an HR professional to play the role of a facilitator. For example, HR acts as a facilitator when training and development activities are planned and conducted and performance appraisals are done.

The Consultant

With the advice of HR specialists the managers resolve problems smoothly, like lack of training, lack of motivation, etc. Thus the HR professional plays the role of an internal management consultant.

The Auditor

Whether the management perform their respective roles concerned with the effective use of human resources or not is determined by an HR specialist.

HR Audit

It is a periodic review to measure the effectiveness of HR management and also to determine further steps for a more effective use of human resources. It is an important aspect of managerial control and is a review and verification of completed transactions to see whether they represent a good state of business affairs or not. The primary aim of HR audit is to determine whether the personnel policies and practices are consistent with organisational objectives. Thus, this audit refers to

(*i*) measurement of effectiveness of the HR management's mission, objectives, strategies and

(*ii*) Determination what should or should not be in the future.

Objectives of HR Audit

According to Gray R. D:

> "The primary aim of personnel audit is to know how different units are functioning and how they meet the policies and guidelines which were agreed upon and assist to rest of the organisation identifying the gap between objectives and results for the end product of an evaluation"

The objectives of HR audit are:

- It reviews the system to acquire, develop, allocate and utilize human resources in the organisation.
- To evaluate the effectiveness of HR staff, policies and practices.
- To evaluate the extent to which line managers have implemented the policies and programs initiated by top management.
- To locate the gaps, shortcomings in the implementation of policies, procedures and directives of the HR department and to know the areas where right / wrong implementation has affected the planned programs and activities.

Need for HR Audit

There is no legal obligation to audit HR policies and practices but some of the modern organisations follow it due to

- To increase the size and personnel of the organisation.
- To change the philosophy of management towards management.
- To increase the strength and influence of trade unions.
- To increase the dependence of the organisation on the HR system and its effective functioning.

Significance of HR Audit

It is used to check the organisational performance in the management of human resources. The significance of HR audit comes to following :

- Employees' participation is essential in organisational activities.
- It provides the required feedback.
- Rising labor costs.
- To avoid the intervention of the government to protect employees interest.

Benefits of HR Audit

- It identifies the contributions of HR department.
- It classifies the HR department's duties and responsibilities.
- It stimulates uniformity of personnel policies and practices.
- It identifies critical personnel problems.
- It reduces human resource costs.

HR Audit Process

It evaluates HR policies, programs, philosophy, practices and compares them with standards prevailing in other different organisations. The level and depth of the audit should be included in advance. According to Rao, the HR audit process has included

- Identify and draw lines, frequency distributions and statistical correlations.
- Examine the variations of different periods and compare them with similar units and industries in the same region.
- Prepare and submit a detailed report to the top management and to the managers for information and necessary action.

Audit Report

There is no prescribed format of the report for HR audit. It is submitted within a reasonable time based on the findings. It examines many aspects of human resource management. HR auditor compiles his observations, analysis and recommendations in the form of a report.

CHALLENGES TO HR PROFESSIONALS

Organisatons to be effective will have to attract, utilize and retain people with knowledge. They should be capable to solve problems, create services, develop new work processes and satisfy customer needs. Knowledge is the most important organisatonal resource. Every company big or small faces five challenges with respect to HR like :

(*a*) **World Business Scenario :** Here, a manager has to deal with a diverse workforce and the consequent complexity. At the same time, the worlforce has to adapt well to the global work environment. It also needs HRM to gain insights about the laws and structure of the countries of operation.

(*b*) **Growth and Profitability :** Organisations in order to be profitable have to attract and retain customers and more and more customer oriented and aim at customer satisfaction. Training in quality and productivity is therefore essential. Companies have to encourage creativity and innovation and free flow of ideas among the employees for a competitive advantage to accelerate achieved growth.

(*c*) **Upgraded Technology :** Managers have to best utilize the available technology. To communicate with employees and top management there are teleconferencing, videoconferencing, and the internet.

(*d*) **Knowledge :** Knowledge is the most important organisational resource and an unlimited and fundamental ingredient for success. It gives competitive advantage to organisations seeking growth. It is essential to attract, develop and retain individuals who add value to the organisation.

(*e*) **Adaptability :** As one of the most difficult challenges a leader has to persuade employees to adjust to changing circumstances and situations.

MODEL QUESTIONS

1. Define the concept and perspectives of human resource management.
2. Explain the development of human resource management.
3. What are the roles of HR executives?
4. Explain the challenges of HR in the present scenario?
5. What do you understand by HR audit?
6. Explain the benefits of HR audit.

CHAPTER

2

Environmental Context of Human Resource Management

An organisation is an open system which needs to interact with the environment for its continuous operation and integrating the activities of the units. So, managers must coordinate the activities of the entire organisation. In doing so, they recognize that an organisation is an element of the larger system consisting of individuals, organisations and institutions that make demand on the organisation because of their dependency and for some valued outcome. To make organisation achieve objectives and survive in the long run, the managers must manage the separate elements of the organisation itself.

There are many resources of an organsiation like men, material, money and machienes. But, the human resource is recognized as the most vital and valuable. Because, the success of an organisation depends upon the quality of human resources and the human resource appreciates in value as it gains more knowledge, experience and efficiency with the passage of time and use, whereas other resources depreciate in value.

Commonly there are two environments that affect organisations operation, like:

- Internal Environment, and
- External Environment

Internal Environment

The major components of internal analysis are resources and competences.

Resource

Any thing, living or dead is put to use for some specific purpose /reason may be seen as a resource depending upon it's use objective and characteristics.

It can be divided into four categories *i.e.*: human resource, financial resource, physical resource (buildings, stock and equipment) and intangible resource(know-how, patent, legal right, brand name, good will).

(*a*) **Human Resource :** The total skills, knowledges, ideas and experiences of the human beings specific to personnel attached to an organisation is human resource and the management of the same is human resource management.

(*b*) **Financial Resource :** These are the assets which are invested by the owner from personal deposits, borrowed from lenders collecting through selling stocks and bonds, that is required to cover operation costs, research and development costs and expansion costs. If an organisation has got enough financial resources to do all these and other financial activities, it is financially strong and can capture any arising opportunities when this financial strength is backed by other organisational resources.

(*c*) **Physical Resource :** It includes buildings, machines and equipments, the location of the organisation for different infrastructural services and layout of offices and plants, these also affect the performance of the organisation. For example, the nature of machineries and equipments(latest or outdated) affect the quality and quantity and cost of products being produced.

(*d*) **Intangible Resource :** Which include knowhow, patent, legal right, reputation and goodwill, brand name also have their own roles to play for organisations smooth, uninterrupted and successful operations. A company known for producing a particular high quality product will have better chance to be successful and get customer for new product it produces with this same brand than that of unknown company.

Competence

It is an attribute or a collection of attributes possessed by most companies in an industry. Without such attributes a business can not survive.

In a company competence can be developed from resources, practical knowledge, skills, technology etc. The competence and core competency in other words is the strong side of the internal organisational variables that makes firms to be competent and if possible be a winner. The result of distinctive capability is an output which customer value higher than competitors. It is based on superior organizational knowledge, information, skill, structure relationship and reputation.

The internal environment reveals the organisation objectives, policies, formal structure and human resource system. The human resource system relates with organisational objectives. So, the quality of human resources must be considered while achieving the goal, because, it is the base of everything right from the objective till the achievement of a goal. In developed countries such as U.S., Canada etc. the quality of human resources is more important than their designations and numbers. The goal of the people is result oriented. In context of an organisation they can do multifarious work apart from the assigned responsibilities. They don't take it otherwise. A manager doesn't need for a subordinate everywhere to assist in his work. For example, if he has to impart training on certain areas he prepares the material, do the typing, arrange the class and also handles different instrument while imparting the training likewise he can perform many works in relation to other tasks, while a person of his stature is not supposed to do that way in other branch of the same company based in our country.

We don't care for the quality. Our only objective is to achieve the position whether we deserve for that or not. In many Indian companies hierarchy is lengthened to accommodate more and more managers whether they are skilled or not. This is the reason we can't make proper objective, policies, formal structures as well as human resource systems.

External Environment

The external environmental forces are those that operate beyond a firm's boundaries and affect its operations. They include economic, demographic, socio-cultural, politico-legal and technological influences. Let us see the impact of these forces one by one :

Economic

(*a*) From the economic point of view human resources has it's importance at national, enterprise and individual levels of analysis. According to Ginzberg, human resources are the key to economic development. But, they are being wasted through unemployment, lack of skills, lack of work opportunities, poor personal practices and the hurdles of change. These resources are responsible for a large part of output and also they have scope for enhancing productivity through their proper development.

(*b*) The *physical resources* can't give results unless the human resources are applied to them. In addition to, if it provides value to physical resources then physical resources can provide a dynamic character to the economy. But, the human resources also have negative aspects. A poorly trained workforce may prove disastrous to the national economy. And, if the national output doesn't increase faster than it's population, the standard of living will decline. Since, it has importance at the enterprise level, so there is urgent need for the effective utilization of human resources to attain the organisational goals. And this can be accomplished by understanding the nature, potentialities and the limitation of these resources, so develop them to their full potential , utilize them to the optimal ability of the enterprise, maintain their quality and amalgate them with other resources.

(*c*) The *core issue* is regarding developing the economic institutions that starts with a government that develops and enforces the law to define and protect the right. Igniting growth and it's sustenation are distinct challenges that requires different sets of policies and approaches. Economic dynamism creates a fertile environment not only for the incumbents but also for the entrants and the new activities.

Business Regulations

Businesses are set of rules , compliance, procedures and a moral and ethical behavioural norms designed to constrain / compel the behaviour of individuals to maximize wealth or utility of principles. Business affects the process of capital accumulation as well as the process of converting this capital into output both of which are key to economic growth and poverty reduction.

The ease of doing business is very important. The cost and time to strart up and close a business are lower in china as compared to other countries in Asia-pacific. According to World Bank report of 2004, it is harder to do business in India than China. Example of this fact is that that in 2004 it took 89 days to start a business in India but it took only 41 days to start a business in China. In addition, India also has more strict labour laws with the result it is much harder to hire and specially fire-workers. This is also an impediment to growth in business. Senior management in Indian firms pay more attention towards the regulatory issues than the management of Chinese firms. The government officials in India who are responsible for overseeing the various rules and regulations have more discretion over what rules and regulation they enforce. With the result they seek higher rent than other developing countries.

Labour Market and Employment

Rigid labour market makes the firm helpless to hire and fire workers in response to shocks to technology, relative prices of outputs and inputs and the macro-economic environment. Moreover, trade reforms needs substantial amount of inter-sectoral labour reallocation as well as intra-sectoral labour reallocation across firms.

Another factor, that has adversely affected the efficiency of the private sector in India is the web of rules that makes restrictions at the entry and the exit of firms. Such restrictions limit the competition that are faced by existing firms and thus lower their efficiency. They also prevent the firms to exit from the market. Thus, the productivity of the industry as a whole gets affected.

Innovation

Indian firms present a full spectrum of technological capabilities. But, there are few firms at international level in terms of product design capability and process technology. Technological capabilities of most of them are inefficient, inferior quality, limited range and high costs. So, they can't face the challenges and the increasing international competition. The major weaknesses are limited R&D capability abd design innovation, low productivity, high capital investment requirement,process capabilities, finishing, safety features, costs, maintenance and operation, marketing and after sales services.There is a need for huge collaboration with global companies so that it could increase competition and a move to adopt total quality management practices.

Human Resources and Knowledge Adaptability

Talent is a crucial factor in implementing any strategy. Talent management is a critical factor for the manufacturer, especially because the demand for qualified labor is more than the supply. In India, manufacturers have to compete with the big IT firms for white collar employees. Attracting, developing and retaining the talent is difficult the world over and is now being difficult in India as well.

Therefore, it is always necessary to upgrade the manpower skills in technical and techno managerial dimension. In a labor-surplus economy, new and efficient technologies are discouraged unless there are sufficient redeployment opportunities.

Service Sector and IT

India's IT industry has flourished with minimum intervention from the Central Government for starting new IT companies the Indian industry did not face major intervention whereas other industries faced major interventions from the Government right from the certification till the establishment. Only, IT industries faced faced limited labor restrictions on hours and over time and received foreign investment for it's development. Whether the Indian government consciously did not regulate IT or only underestimated it's possible growth is unclear but it's growth has been helped by the Government as compared to other companies.

Demographic

These are outcomes of changes in or changing attitude towards the characteristics of population such as age, gender, ethic, origin, race, sexual orientation and social class. Like the other forces, it presents managers with opportunities and threats and can have major implications for organisations.There are many factors responsible for the change into their composition like labor force, social mobility, education, evolving social and political climate in the countries.

With the result, higher skills and educational requirements has made visible the traditional distinction between manual and non-manual workers. Employees are seeking and demanding parity in employee's benefits among different categories and levels. Earlier, women has been recruited mainly as labor in agriculture and related traditional industries like plantations etc. now they increasingly occupying white collar and managerial positions.

Socio-cultural

These are the pressures emanating from the social structure of a country or society or from the national culture. Social structure is the arrangement of relationship between individuals and groups in a society. Societies differ substantially in social structure. In societies that have a high degree of social stratification, there are many distinctions among individuals and groups. The socio-cultural dimensions of the environment consists of factors like customs, life styles and values that characterize the society in which the firms operates and it influences the firms to obtain it's resources, makes its goods and services and function within the society. Population changes, rising educational levels, norms, values and attitudes towards social responsibility are examples of socio-cultural variables.

Population Changes

The changes in population have many consequences for organisations. As, the total population changes, the demand for products and services also change. For example, the decline in the birthrate and improvement in healthcare have increased the average age of the population in the united states. Many firms that marketed their products toward youths are developing the productlines so that it may appeal to an older market. Firms are developing the product lines so that it may appeal to an older market. Firms are developing strategies that will allow them to capitalize on the aging population.

Rising Educational Levels

The rising educational levels enables people to earn more than otherwise also, the increased expectations of workers and the job mobility. If there income is more naturally they can purchase additional goods and services and it will support to raise the overall standard of living of a large segment of the population. Now, workers are not accepting undesirable working conditions that were a generations ago with the workers.

Norms and Values

Norms (standard accepted forms of behaviour) and values (aptitudes toward right and wrong) differ across time and between geographical area. Lifestyles differ among different ethnic groups. Examples, customers expect increasing quality in products.

Social Responsibility

A business or individual should strive to improve the welfare of the society. Norms and values what is considered socially responsible for behaviour that changes over time. During the early part of the twenty first century prominent social values and human rights were environmental quality (most prominent, recycling and waste reduction) in addition to general social welfare.

Stakeholders are anyone with a stake in the organsiation existence. They think to incorporate socially responsible issue into a firms strategies. To maximize the return to stakeholders decision may be taken to close an unprofitable plant.

Politico-legal

These result from political and legal developments within society and significantly affect managers and organisations. The legal environment defines what organisations can not do at a particular point of time.

Attitudes Towards Business

If the govt. has pro business attitude then it enables firm to enter into business practices. Smoking and it's related risks alters the public's attitude. So limiting to smoking to workplace or designated area is a necessity to bring changes in the organisation.

Legislation

In India various laws and acts, formulated and amended over the years such as – Trade Union Act (1926), The Industrial Employment (Standing Order) Act (1957), Payment of Wages Act (1946), The Factories Act (1948), Payment of Gratuity Act (1972) etc. have shaped and tuned the spirit of Indian organisations and the workforce. The legal environment is becoming more complex and affecting businesses more directly. It has become difficult for businesses to take action without encountering a law, regulation or legal problem.

Levels of Government Influence

Government policies and programmes affect the way market operates. Regulation concerning to many business practices differ between the states and the tax rates vary widely.

Government may provide incentives to attract business to the area, may build industrial parks, service roads and provide low interest bonds to encourage a desirable business to move into the community.

Technological

Technological forces are outcomes of changes in the technology that managers use to design, produce or distribute goods and services. Technological innovations bring changes because they are not just changes in the way the work is performed. Instead, the innovation process promotes associated changes in the work relationships and organisation structures. Sophisticated information technology is also making organisations more responsive. The team approach adopted by many organisations lead to flatter structures, decentralised decision-making and a more open communication among the leaders and team members.

Demand

Changing technology affects the demand for a firm's product and services, it's production processes and raw materials. It can change the life-style and buying patterns of consumers.

Developments in the field of micro-computers have created opportunities for businesses to engage in business via Internet. Earlier computers were used only by large organisations to handle data processing needs, now personal computers are being used by smaller firms and individuals that was not imagined fifteen years ago. Similarly, new developments in technology have reduced prices of computers and expanded to the general public rather than to business, scientific and professional users.

Technology has removed certain products from the market. A number of chemicals that have been used by farmers to control insets or plants that are prohibited from use or require licensure as a consequence of those chemicals appearing the food chain.

Production Processes

Technology also changes production methods. Example-robotics, represents one of the most visible challenges to the existing production methods.

When production was first automated, some workers were displaced, new jobs were created to maintain the auto mated equipment.

Evaluating Technological Changes

Technology, represents both, potential threats and potential opportunities for the established products. Products with new technology are often introduced but it is hard to assess their market potential. When ball-point pens were first introduced they leaked, skipped and left large blotches of ink on the writing surface. Fountain pen manufacturers believed that new technology was not a threat to existing products and can't attempt to produce ball-point pens until substantial market share of fountain pen could be lost.

It is quite difficult to predict the impact of new technology on an existing product, still the need to monitor the environment for new technological developments is obvious.

MODEL QUESTIONS

1. Analyse the environment of human resource management.
2. What factors have hindered the progress of human resource management?
3. What has resulted with socio cultural factors in the society?

CHAPTER 3

Corporate Objectives and Human Resource Planning

Concept

Objectives are the key to effective planning. In fact, planning has no meaning unless it is related to certain well-defined objectives or goals. These are not only useful in planning but also in other managerial functions like planning, organising, directing and controlling. They are an important aid in decision-making in any area of business.

It measures the performance of various people working in the organisation and the overall effectiveness and efficiency of the organisation.

According to Ordiorne : MBO (Management by Objectives) is not only a set of rules, a series of procedures or even a set method of managing, but it a way of thinking about management. It is also known as management by results.

According to Dale D. Mc.Conkey : the term management by results has been preferred by him and he has defined it as an approach to management planning and evaluation in which specific targets for a year or some other length of time are established for each amanger on the basis of results which each must achieve if the overall objectives of the company are to be realized. At the end of this period, the actual results achieved are measured against the original goal.

Types of Objectives

Generally, big enterprises have both major and derivative objectives. Major objectives are set up for the entire organisation. They are broader in scope and are applicable throughout the enterprise. They are also known as primary objectives. Derivative objectives are drived from the major objectives of the enterprise. Every department draws it's specific objectives in order to contribute to the major goals of the enterprise. They are known as departmental objectives and are subsidiary to the main objectives of the enterprise.

Hirarchy of Objectives

The objectives of a company can be structured into a hierarchy. The objectives at the lower levels are the means for the higher levels. If we go down the hierarchy, we shall find that the major objective followed by different departments focuses on creating the form of specialised machine tools. At the next level, there may be intermediate objectives concerned with manufacturing and assembling the major components. At the lowest level, the objective of the individuals consists of performing the detailed work on sub components parts. The mentioned example explains the fact that the objectives at different levels in the company are integrated and follow a logical sequence as reflected by it's organisation chart. Each operation has a specific objective which must contribute to the overall objective. The objective at the top level provides the basis for setting the objective at the second level which in turn becomes the basis for objective at the third and so on.

Multiplicity of Objectives

It is wrong to say that there can be only one objective of an organisation. To manage a business is to balance a variety of needs and goals, and this requires multiple objectives.

Peter Drucker has suggested the following eight key areas in which objectives must be set :

(*i*) Marketing, (*ii*) Innovation (*iii*) Human Organisation (*iv*) Financial resources (*v*) Physical resources (*vi*) productivity (*vii*) Social responsibility (*viii*) Profit requirements.

Objectives in these areas helps the management :

- to organise and explain the whole range of business
- to test the objectives in actual experience
- to predict behaviour
- to appraise the soundness of decisions while they are still being made
- to set managers on all levels to analyse their experience and improve their performance.

Benefits of MBO

- It moulds planning, directing and controlling in a number of ways.
- It stimulates meaningful action for better performance and higher accomplishment.
- It is closely associated with the concept of decentralisation because decentralization cannot work without the support of management by objectives.
- When applied consciously and systematically it leads to stimulating subordinates motivation, serving as device for organsiational control and integration, locating weak and problem areas, analyzing training needs etc.

Process of MBO

The process of managing by objectives sets organisational goals and the goals of different divisions and sub-divisions. It is a continuous process which not only ensures sustained centralisation of efforts towards organisatioanl objectives, but also helps in modifying objectives to suit the changed situation. The steps in MBO are :

(*i*) **Setting of Objectives :** In order to set objectives of the enterprise a detailed assessment is made at different resources at it's disposal. A market survey is conducted to know what types of goods and services are required by the community. Proper forecasts is made to estimate the demand and the business conditions in the country. This detailed analysis leads to highliting of desirable objectives, both long range and short range. An attempt is made to set specific golas in various key areas on which the survival and growth of the business depends. These objectives the top management try to achieve and determines the objectives of every department. At this stage, the top management discuss the objectives with the departmental maangers to find agreed statement. Each department sets both long range and short range objectives with the approval of top management.

(ii) **Revision of Organisation Structure :** After resetting the goals of each individual under MBO a considerable change in the job descriptions of various position is taken up. This may need for a revision of the existing organsiation structure. The organisation charts and manuals is suitably amended to depict the change brought by the introduction of management by objectives (MBO). The job description of various jobs define their objectives, responsibilities and authorities and the relationship with other job positions in the organsiation.

(iii) **Establishing Check-points :** Management by objectives ensures periodic meetings between the superior and the subordinate to review the progress towards the accomplishment of targets of the subordinate. The superior establish check points or standards of performance to evaluate the progress of the subordinate. The standards should be defined quantitatively as far as possible and the subordinate must understand them. The key result analysis should be reduced into writing and should contain the following information :

- the overall objectives of the job of the subordinate
- the key results he must achieve to fulfil his objectives.
- The long term and short term priorities of tasks he must adhere to.
- Appraisal of performance.

The important benefit of MBO is that it sets asides the judgemental role of the supervisor. The performance of every individual is evaluated in terms of the end results agreed by the superior or the subordinate.

Concept of HRP

Human Resource Planning (HRP) basically ensures the availability of right resources in the right place to match the future organisational needs. The process of human resource planning is the key to the organisation, if it is done carefully and based on real and factual data available.

It can be defined as the process of ensuring the right number of qualified people, into the right job, at the right time, to deliver the results in an efficient and effective manner. It is the system of matching available resources, either internally or externally with the demand that the organisation expects to have over a period of time. Available internal resources are the employees who are already in the organisation and the external resources are those who have to be recruited from outside.

The process of human resource planning starts with understanding organisational objectives and translating them into a schedule of employee requirements over a period of time. The next step is to devise plans to secure the right resources to meet these requirements. It is the responsibility of the HR department to ensure a balance in the management of human resources in an unstable and unpredictable market. For example, many IT and BPO firms in India make job offers to a large number of graduates but are unable to attract and retain the talent. It means a proper human resource management system is required. Human resource planning is also called manpower planning, employment planning or personal planning.

OBJECTIVES OF HUMAN RESOUCE PLANNING

The objectives of human resource planning are:

(*i*) To develop the existing human resources.

(*ii*) To utilize and maintain the quantity and quality human resources effectively and efficiently

(*iii*) To maintain the required quantity and quality of human resources.

(*iv*) To forecast the turnover/ attrition rates.

(*v*) To plan to meet organisational human resource needs.

(*vi*) To foresee the effects of technological changes.

(*vii*) To optimize staffing in the organisation.

(*viii*) To estimate the value of human resources.

Importance of Human Resource Planning

- It identifies existing manpower gaps so that available training programmes may be developed in terms of their quality and quantity.
- human resource planning creates awareness about the right man in the right place because man is required in relation to work.
- It ensures that adequate number of persons are selected and trained well in advance to fill future job vacancies in the organisation and also may be replaced if needed.
- It facilitates the expansion and diversification of business in respect of assessing future requirements of the company expansion and new units set up.
- It is helpful in effective utilisation of technological progress.

Human Resources Planning at Different Planning Levels

Human resource planning is done at various levels in the organisation to meet the resource requirements. The flow of communication regarding HRP has to be both ways that is from top to bottom and from bottom to top.

Corporate-level Planning

This level takes into consideration the changing market situation, strategic plans of the organisation, the technological changes anticipated etc.

So, the role of human resource planning is to identify the broad policy issues relating to human resources.

Intermediate-level Planning

Intermediate-level planning is done at the strategic business unit level. The human resource planning at this stage is done based on the corporate level human resource plan and at this level it includes determining the recruitment/lay off strategy, retaining strategy etc.

Operations Planning

Like other planning levels, these are made in pursuit of the organisational objectives. These include simple plans like plans like recruitment, training and development of resources etc.

THE REOCESS OF HUMAN RESOURCE PLANNING

It involves planning for long-term needs, and takes into consideration the career planning for individual employees and succession planning in the organisation. The basic step of human resource planning are :

Assessment of Human Resources

If the assessment of the human resource is completed, an inventory of human resources can be prepared in terms of the knowledge, skill set and qualifications and other HR activities like training and development, career planning and succession planning.

With the help of job analysis it provides the basis for the assessment of an organisation's current human resource situation. Also, their clarity in terms of the work that needs to be done and the resources available to the work.

Forecasting the Demand and Supply of Labour

The future demand of manpower are compared with the current availability of resources and it is assessed accordingly whether there would be a deficit or a surplus in the future.

For this different forecasting methods like time series analysis, regression analysis and productivity ratios are used to determine future human resource requirements

If, more engineers are expected to be easily available in the job market after four years, it may be more beneficial to employ engineers than technicians. Similarly, if dramatic changes in technology are expected, the human resource needs may become completely different so human resource planning has to take into consideration all these aspects before forecasting the demand and working on an action plan.

Matching the Inventory with Future Requirements

If the current inventory exceeds the future demand of manpower, then redeployment or retrenchment is considered.

If, the current inventory falls short of the future demand for manpower, there are two possibilities either train the existing employees to meet the future requirement or plan for recruitment. At every point the costs and the time involved have to be evaluated.

MANAGING THE FORECASTED DEMAND/SURPLUS (REDEPLOYMENT)

The prepared action plan is properly phased out after matching the human resource inventory with the future needs. Say, if there is a requirement of 10 engineers in the production department by the beginning of the fourth quarter, it would not make much sense to find out competent and experienced engineers at the beginning of the first quarter itself. If they are recruited at the beginning of the first quarter itself the organisation will have to pay them for nine months, so, while analyzing the future requirements in comparison to the current inventory, the following sources of supply must be considered as :

- Promotions, transfer and demotions also have an effect on the human resource plan.
- Addition of new-hires, who join the organisation from outside.
- Transfers, which may not affect the organisational balance.
- Employees going on long leave or coming back after a long leave.
- Separations from the organisation due to retirement, resignation, death or sickness.
- The political, social and legal environment also have an influence on the external supply of human resources.

Managing Future Demand

A decision has to be taken whether to employ permanent or temporary staff, if there is requirement of more human resources. The area of demand and the skill set required is also to be considered while planning for recruitment. Example, it may be forecasted that there is requirement of two engineers in the production department and one of these positions may need a working knowledge of finance. Such nuances have to be considered while planning an intake of employees.

Managing Future Surplus

In some cases, the surplus manpower can be deployed in other projects or units, to avoid the confusion involved in a permanent separation.

If the organisation cannot afford the surplus/excess manpower for too long, suitable action like a voluntary retirement scheme or a golden handshake may be considered.

Retrenchment

It means either the employer cannot offer the employee any alternative position, or any alternative position offered by the employer is not accepted by the employee. It is usually permanent.

Outplacement

Organisations which are employee friendly, but considering to reduce their manpower, may provide outplacement services to their surplus employees. They search for other employment opportunities for their displaced employees and offer them assistance in getting new jobs. This assistance to the employees may be in terms of preparing the resumes and preparing for interviews etc.

Lay-offs

Most of the organisations resort to lay-offs when the demand for their products or services have gone down and the supply cannot be maintained at the existing levels. Temporary lay offs were common till a few decades back and are still prevalent in the unorganized sector.

Leave of Absence without Pay

It is one of the methods of temporary cost cutting at the time of crisis. The organisations take the help of this method when they undergo some major changes.

Loaning

During slack periods it is a suitable option when the organisations do not want their middle/top level managers to stagnate, or leave the company. They loan their managers for a specified period of time to other organisations, usually government or quasi-government.

Work Sharing

It is another concept by which loyal and dedicated workers can be retained in the company even during slack periods. This is suitable for the employees at the operational levels and lower levels of management.

Reduced Work Hours

This is one of the popular techniques employed to avoid retrenchment/lay-off and is again suitable at lower levels of management.

Early / voluntary Retirement

Early/voluntary retirement is one of the techniques of getting rid/releasing of ageing employees and infusing fresh talent into the organisation. This can also be used as a downsizing technique. This is a very popular downsizing tool in many of the public sector companies, and other organisations in India.

Attrition

Attrition is the separation of employees from an organisation, due to resignation, retirement etc.

MODEL QUESTIONS

1. Explain objectives with different types.
2. What is multiplicity of objectives and how it is helpful for the management?
3. What are the processes of objectives and how it is useful?
4. What are the processes of human resource planning?
5. What is redeployment and how it takes place?

CHAPTER 4

Job Analysis and Design

Concept of Job Analysis

Job analysis is a collection of data. It consists of task , duties, responsibilities which as a whole is regar7ded as an assignment to individual employees.

It is the process by which the tasks which comprise the job are determined and the skills and abilities required to perform it successfully are identified. It is also known as job study or work study. It involves:

- Preparing job description, job specification, job requirements and employee specification so that the HR manager could determine the nature, levels and quantum of human resources required.
- Providing guides, plan and the basis for job design and redesign.
- While training employees for a particular position the parameters on which the employees need to be trained can be obtained by it, also helps in designing and managing performance appraisal system. Thus, directly or indirectly it contributes to all the fields of HRM.

According to Flippo "It is the process of studying and collecting information relating to the operations and responsibilities of a specific job."

Objectives of Job Analysis

The objectives of job analysis are as follows:

- Simplification in work,
- Establishing work standards, and
- Support of other personal activities.

Job Analysis Information

The job analysis provides the following information :

- Job identification which includes job title.
- Signifying characteristics of a job including location, physical setting, supervision, union jurisdiction, hazards, etc.
- What the typical worker will do ?
- How the job is performed ?
- What materials and equipments the worker uses ?
- Job relationship.

Uses/Advantages/Benefits of Job Analysis

- It helps to improve efficiency due to better placement and frequently suggests methods for improvements.
- It helps in improving the design of the jobs and work methods. Also, in analyzing work processes and work simplification.
- It helps in devising the training and development programmes for employees.
- It helps management in the proper allocation of authority and responsibility by describing the duties of each job and inter-relationships among jobs.
- It facilitates job evaluation and job performance appraisal which are necessary for wage determination, for appraising the working conditions and promotions and transfers.
- It gives us two important segments *i.e.,* job description and job specification - on the basis of which job evaluation process is done.

- It is used to solve industrial disputes and to maintain sound industrial relations.
- It is essential to plan the careers of individual employees and prepare them to progress along their career paths.
- It involves identifying and grooming a successor for a vacancy that would arise in the future.

PROCESS OF JOB ANALYSIS

The process of analyzing a job consists of:

Information Gathering

This is the first step in job analysis. This includes information about organisation structure, the role of the job in relation to other jobs in the organisation; the class to which the job belongs, and a detailed description of the activities and responsibilities involved in the job. This information is collected through observation and study.

Job-Specific Competency Determination

Based on study and observation, the competencies required for the job are identified.

Developing a Job Description

Details of the tasks, responsibilities, duties and functions of the job are prepared. Combining all these forms the job description.

Developing a Job Specification

It provides a complete list of competencies and qualifications required to match the job description. This is also prepared based on study, comparison or direct inputs from the job-holders.

JOB ANALYSIS METHODS

Different methods of job analysis can be broadly classified as:

Observation Method

This method is simple and can be used with other methods of job analysis. When individuals perform the job their performance is observed and relevant points are noted. These include the notes about what was done and how it was done. This method has some serious drawbacks. For jobs which are not repetitive but complicated, it is difficult to make a note of the observations. This problem can be tackled by work sampling. The observer knows what has to be noted and what has to be ignored. Otherwise, the whole analysis may be a lengthy and redundant document.

Individual Interview Method

This method is used when the job is complex and has varied tasks. It is effective when the interview is structured and the analyst is clear about what information has to be obtained from the interview.

Group interview Method

Information that has been missed out in individual interviews can come up in a group interview. This method is also less time consuming. Drawback of this method is the effect that group dynamics may have on the direction of the interview.

Questionnaire Method

In this method, the analyst gives a long and structured questionnaire to be filled up by the job-holders. This questionnaire has both objective and open-ended questions. It is a good method to get the information from the employee without disturbing him on the job. Analyst might fail to convey what he intends to and in the process fail to obtain the required information. The disadvantage of this method is that such a list can never be completely exhaustive.

Technical Conference Method

This is a method of gathering all the job-related information from 'experts'-usually supervisors-and not the job-holders.

More and unbiased information can be gathered from the experts but the view point of the job holder cannot be obtained.

Diary Method

In this method job holders/incumbents make note of the activities they perform. This exercise takes longer to complete as there may be activities that occur at long time intervals. For example, an office assistant may have the responsibility of sending a monthly attendance report to the headquarters. This activity may be missing from his list of responsibilities if performed at the end of every month for a shorter period.

Functional Job Analysis

Functional Job analysis was developed by the U.S. Department of Labour. In this method, the job analyst conducts research, interviews of job holders/incumbents and supervisors, makes site observations and then prepares a detailed document. The work functions of any job can be categorized under the headings of data, people, and things.

Position Analysis Questionnaire (PAQ)

It generates job requirement information that is applicable to all types of jobs and contains 194 job elements that fall into six major job categories.

By analyzing 194 job elements for more than 500 different jobs, researchers identified the following important dimensions on which jobs differed from one another:

(*i*) **Having decision-making/communications/ social responsibilities :** The activities that involve communication and interaction with people, as well as decision-making functions are part of this dimension.

(*ii*) **Performing skilled activities :** The activities that involve technical devices and in which the emphasis is on precision, recognising differences, manual control are part of this dimension.

(*iii*) **Being Physically Active/Related Environmental Conditions :** The activities that involve movement of the entire body or major parts of it.

(*iv*) **Operating Vehicles/Equipment :** The activities that use vehicles or equipment and involve sensory and perceptual processes are a part of this dimension.

(*v*) **Processing Information :** The activities that involve a wide range of information-processing exercises.

Critical Incident Technique (CIT)

According to John Flanagan who proposed the Critical Incident Technique in 1954, behaviours in specific situation contribute to the success or failure of individuals or organisations. A compilation of all the behaviours provides a rough picture of the job that focus on both the action of the worker and the context in which the behavior was noticed.

The CIT is suitable for middle and top management level jobs as it can take place at these levels. So, this technique is limited to a few people and its application is restricted to routine jobs at the lower levels of an organisation structure.

ISSUES IN JOB ANALYSIS

In some organisations, job analysis is used by the management for down-sizing or for re-evaluating jobs for wage administration.

To be successful, the first problem associated with job analysis is that it needs the support and involvement of various sections of the organisation like the employees, the management, the unions, and of course the HR department. It is important to assess employee's fear communicating all the details of the exercise in a simple and transparent manner.

The second problem associated with job analysis is the need to update the information gathered. Job descriptions and specifications may change as the changes take place in the organisational structure. For example, a new job may come up due to changes in organisational structure or processes. Thus, updating the information becomes essential. Two methods can be used to deal with this issue. One method is used to ask supervisors to make an annual review of the changes that have occurred and incorporate these in the job analysis information. The second method is to have managers convey the proposed changes in jobs. Once, the changes are made with relation to any job, these may be updated in the job analysis information. The second method is less time-consuming more effective as changes are incorporated immediately and not at the end of the year.

JOB DESCRIPTION

Job description describes in detail the various aspects of a job like the tasks involved, the responsibilities of the job and the deliverables. Also, describes the setting and the work environment of the job. It is used in recruitment, training, performance appraisal and wage and salary administration.

Drafting and Maintaining Job Description

The following guidelines help in writing a good job description:

(*i*) The nature and scope of the work including all important relationships.

(*ii*) The work and duties of the position should be clearly explained/laid out.

(*iii*) To show the kind of work, the degree of complexity, the degree of skill required, the degree and type of accountability.

(*iv*) Supervisory responsibility.

A new employee should identify the job description that can help in understanding the job and its basic requirements.

As the operations in an organisation keep changing in response to market demand and technological changes likewise job and their descriptions also change. So, job descriptions must be updated as and when major changes take place in responsibilities, relationships or tasks.

JOB SPECIFICATION

A job specification is a written statement of the minimum acceptable qualifications, knowledge, skills, traits, physical and mental characteristics that a job holder must posses to perform the job successfully. These specifications are:

(*i*) **Physical characteristics :** height, weight, vision, voice etc.

(*ii*) **Personal characteristics :** emotional stability, good and pleasing manners, way of dealing with others.

(*iii*) **Psychological characteristics :** analytical ability, mental concentration and alertness.

(*iv*) **Responsibilities :** responsibility for generating confidence, trust and for others safety.

To prepare a complete and correct job specifications is difficult as compared with preparing correct job description. Because there is disagreement concerning the human requirement for work moreover whether the requirement should mandatory or desirable.

CONCEPT OF JOB DESIGN

Job design is the process of structuring work and designating the specific activities at individual or group levels. Job design determines the responsibility of an employee, the authority he enjoys over his work, his scope of decision-making and, his level of satisfaction and productivity. Satisfaction and productivity are interrelated and inter-dependent. Job design also has an effect on the relationships and the productivity in a group.

It is a complex process that must be viewed from several point of views such as organisational goals, employee aspirations, performance standards and work environment are some of the major factors that need to be taken into consideration in job design.

Job content includes the various tasks or activities that have to be performed by the job-holder, he responsibilities attached to the job and the relationships with other jobs in the organisational set-up.

Different Approaches to Job Design

Different approaches to job design have been proposed over the years. While the earlier approaches concentrated just on the 'technical' aspect and ignored the 'human' aspect, the later approaches paid attention to 'human aspect'.

Frederick W. Taylor developed engineering approach that gave rise to the engineering approach to job design. The key element of this approach was the 'task idea'. The 'task idea' is the work of every workman that is fully planned and laid out by the management, at least one day in advance. The workers are given specific instructions what is to be done, how it is to be done and the exact time to be taken to complete the work.

According to principles of scientific management, the role of management in job design is as follows:

1. The manager determines the one best way to perform the job.
2. The manager employs the individuals according to their abilities.
3. The manager undertakes planning, organising and controlling of a job.

The engineering approach was very popular for many years, as it had many advantages. Management could hire unskilled labor force for almost all operative job in the organisation but these job were designed for people with limited skills or experience. Though specialization offered economic benefits and organisational performance but workers felt that over specialisation hindered the development of interpersonal relationships with the managers as well as co-workers.

Some of the Demerits of Over Specialisation

Repetition : Performing the same tasks repeatedly resulted in boredom.

Mechanical pacing : All the workers had to work continuously at a predetermined pace.

No. End product: Due to over specialisation, employees were manufacturing bits and pieces and not producing any identifiable end product.

Little social interaction : Employees had limited chances of interacting on a casual basis with their co-workers.

No personal input: Lack of personal control over the job in the terms of choosing the methods by which the job were to be performed.

Modern Management Techniques

In the recent past, organisations have deviated from traditional work schedules and polices in order to motivate the employees to perform efficiently and effectively and HR initiatives have also helped in enhancing/increasing the human resources of an organisation and enriching the quality of work life for the employees. Some of the recent trends in job design are.

Job Rotation

Job rotation enhances employee motivation assigning the employee to alternative jobs. The employee gain a wider knowledge of the organisation and its work processes. It helps managers to deal frequent absenteeism and high turnover of workforce. It is also an effective technique of training new and inexperienced employees. Moreover, it helps in developing management generalists at higher organisational levels.

Job Enlargement

Job enlargement increases length and operating time of each cycle of work for the job-holder. It reduces the number of repetitions of the operating cycle and increases the scope of work for the employee. It gives a sense of satisfaction to the employee as his end product is more significant when compared to end product in the earlier, shorter cycle.

It increases the scope and depth of the job. Its application is different from that of job enlargement.

Job Enrichment

It is the most popular technique for enhancing employee motivation. It is done by redesigning jobs to increase their scope and depth.

It caters to all the job characteristics mentioned in the 'job characteristics approach' to job design. The support and commitment of the top management is essential to train and counsel managers to adapt to the new style of working which has low power and control. They also should be trained in providing timely and productive feedback to the employees. The employees also need to be equipped to handle an enriched job independently.

The example of an enriched job in today's context is of a Sales Manager in consumer durables firm. He has to identify the customer, understand their needs provide/customize the product service if required, market the product to them, maintain contact with them for the after-sales service. Manager is free to take any decision he may like to satisfy the customer. He is also encouraged to be creative and innovative in his job.

Job Enrichment Techniques

Techniques of job enrichment are given below :

(*i*) Incorporating more responsibility in the job.

(*ii*) Providing wider scope, greater sequencing and increased pace of work

(*iii*) Assigning a natural unit of work.

(*iv*) Minimizing controls and providing freedom of work.

(*v*) Concentrating on motivational factors like achievement, responsibility, self control.

(*vi*) Changing the content of the job rather than changing the employees.

MODEL QUESTIONS

1. Explain the process of job analysis.
2. What are the methods of job analysis and how it is useful?
3. Write notes on: job design, job specification, job rotation and job enlargement.
4. Explain modern management techniques.

CHAPTER 5

Recruitment

Concept

It is necessary to have a well-defined recruitment policy so that it could respond quickly with the changing business environment.

The magnitude of recruitment and the methods to be used are determined by human resource plan. Depending on human resource planning a organisation decides on the number of people to recruit, the jobs for which to recruit, and whether the recruitment is for permanent or temporary staff. Once these decisions are made, the modes of recruitment are finalised.

After finalising the process of manpower planning the next step is to hire the personnel according to the requirements. So related to this there are questions *i.e.,* where to hire, when to hire, who is to hire, hiring should be from within or outside, what should be the media or source and finally how they should be hired.All these questions are responded properly when a company is having a suitable and appropriate personnel policies and procedures. Recruitment which is the most important function of human resource management makes it possible to acquire the number and types of people necessary to ensure the continued operation of the organisation.

Recruitment forms the first stage in the process which continues with selection and ceases with the placement of the candidate. It is the discovering of potential applicants for actual or anticipated organisational vacancies.

Though employment, recruitment and selection are used inter-changeably, technically all the three have different meanings. Recruitment and selection together constitute employment. It is the process of seeking and attracting prospective candidates against a vacancy in an organisation. It involves:

- Identifying or creating new sources of applicants.
- Extracting the existing sources of applicants and developing the new sources.
- Stimulating and attracting the candidates to apply for jobs in an organisation.
- Deciding the recruitment procedure.

Responsible Factors for Recruitment

There are many factors that affect the recruitment programme. These factors can be classified as organisational or internal factors and environmental or external actors.

Organisational Factors/ Internal Factors

There are several factors that influence the success or failure of a recruitment programme. Some of these are described below.

1. A major factor that explores/determines the success of a recruitment programme is the reputation of the organisation. An organisation's reputation depends on size, area of business, profitability, management, etc. in addition to its philosophy and values. For example, a profitable firm famous for its strong values has a better response to a recruitment drive than a loss-making firm known for its lack of values.
2. The organisational culture and the attitude of its management towards employees also influence a candidate's decision to apply for an organisation. An

organisation that is known for employee-friendly policies is certainly preferred over an orthodox and rigid organisation.

3. Another factor that contributes to the success of a recruitment programme is geographical location of the vacant position. Prospective candidates may not be too eager to work in a remote place unless they belong to that place.
4. The amount of resources allocated also determines the success of a recruitment drive. For example, if a critical position in an organisation needs to be filled up in a month's time, the substantial resources may have to be allocated to the task. In contrast, if a non-critical position is to be filled up in three months time, the substantial resources may not have to be allocated too much to the task.
5. The methods and channels used to advertise the vacancy also determine success of a recruitment program.
6. The perks/emoluments that the company offers influence the decision of a candidate.

Environmental Factors/External Environment

Apart from the organisational factors some external factors also determine effectiveness of a recruitment programme.

1. The situation in the labor market, the demand for manpower, the demographics, the knowledge and the skill set available - all determine the response to a recruitment program. For example, today there are more fresh engineering graduates available in the job market than ever before. Therefore, a firm looking for fresh engineering graduates may get a phenomenal response.
2. The stage of development of the industry to which the organisation belongs also influences the results of a recruitment programme.

3. Attitudes, beliefs and culture also impact the effectiveness of a recruitment programme. For example, a pharmacy company may attract more talent than a cigarette manufacturing company, in a culture which has strong values and traditions.
4. The law of the land and the legal implications involved also design a recruitment programme determining its effectiveness.

Policy for Recruitment

Usually, the recruitment policy is in accordance with the objectives and policies of the organisation. It lays down the objectives of recruitment and the channels and sources of recruitment.

According to Yoder, the recruitment policy emphasises on the quantity and qualifications of manpower. An efficient and demanding recruitment policy:

(*i*) Is designed in such a way that ensures long-term employment opportunities for its employees and avoids frequent lay-offs.

(*ii*) Is in alignment with the objectives and people policies of the organisation.

(*iii*) Complies with government policies on hiring.

(*iv*) Assures the candidates of the management's interest in their development.

(*v*) Prevents the formation of small groups.

(*vi*) Reflects the social commitment of the organisation.

(*vii*) Is flexible enough to accommodate changes in the organisation.

(*viii*) Is cost effective for the organisation.

A successful recruitment policy is based on organisation's objectives, recruitment needs, preferred sources of recruitment, criteria for selection, cost of recruitment and other financial implications. It should reflect the reputation and image of the organisation.

SOURCES OF RECRUITMENT

If an organisation is looking for a young fresh technician, it would be better to advertise in the local newspapers. Similarly, if an organisation needs fresh talent in large numbers, then organisation team must visit to some of the best colleges. As it will be more beneficial than advertising in newspapers or magazines.

Different sources of recruitment can be employed depending on various factors like the level of the position, the number of people required, time available and the funds allocated for recruitment. The different sources of recruitment are internal search, advertisements, employee reference, employment agencies, educational institutes and interested applicants.

Internal Search

Organisations which decides go in for an internal search consider present employees as candidates for openings. Promotion from within can help build morale and keep high quality employees from leaving the firm.

The policy of developing employees from inside instead of searching for new talents from outside has various advantages.

- It maintains good employer-employee relations and boosts the morale of the employees.
- It encourages competent and ambitious individual.
- The cost, time and resources are saved on the selection and induction processes.
- If handled properly promoting from within can also act as a training and development device for middle and top level management.

The disadvantages of internal search: Talents available in the market may miss out by the organisation. Also, possible that the talents already available in the organisation may stagnate without fresh inflows from outside. Because, when the new employees are recruited from outside it may rejuvenate the systems and processes of the organisation providing fresh perspectives and ideas.

External Sources

There are various methods of recruiting from external sources such as advertisements, campus recruitments, employee referrals, employment exchanges, private placement agencies, etc. Moreover, a job preview method that provides the applicant with real requirements of the job that the organisation is trying to achieve is deirable.

Advertisements

The medium of advertisement depends upon different factors such as the cost, need, nature of the job, its level and criticality in the organisation. In some companies television and radio is also used as other media for job advertisements.

Mostly, organisations use print media to advertise but sometimes resort to blind advertisements. They do not want their competitors to know about a critical position vacant. Also, to avoid responding to all the participants for the position.

Some organisations like to announce the pay package in the advertisement while others do not prefer not it. As pay packages vary for the middle and higher level management cadres, they like to finalize it only after determining the worth of the applicant. In some cases, like public sector units in India, where the company has a "fixed pay policy, there is no hesitation in disclosing the pay for a position.

Many companies and individuals use different internet portals such as naukri.com, monsterindia.com and jobsahead.com who are in search of a suitable job. These days, many organisations maintain their own websites which load their vacancies for the visitors on the website with important informations.

The important information that has to be given in an advertisement includes:

- Nature of business and size of the organisation
- The nature of the job
- Requirements of the job in terms of qualification, experience, knowledge and skills.
- Emoluments, perks and benefits
- Location or place of work
- Tasks and responsibilities
- Reporting hierarchy
- Last date and ways to respond - by e-mail, telephone or post

Employee Referrals

Employees working with an organisation recommend their friends or relatives for vacant positions in the organisation. They gather information from the employees regarding vacant positions and provide suitable candidate in against of the vacancy so they have greater expectations from the company. Thus they have more possibility of his continuing in the job. Another advantage of referrals is in terms of time and cost savings for the organisation. There are some disadvantages also to this system. Sometimes, employees refer relatives or friends, who may not be suitable for the job. It may also lead to the formation of groups in the organisation with the members of the same group.

Employment Agencies

The employment agencies are broadly classified as public or state agencies, private agencies and head hunters.

In search of suitable employment fresh pass outs register themselves with the local employment exchange. The employment exchange facilitates communication between the candidates and the company.

Private agencies or 'management consultants' provides suitable candidates to the company at the junior, middle and management level. They perform all the initial phases of interview like- they invite applications from interested candidates, scan them for the first round of short listing, test them or interview them for a second round of short listing and finally make the list of the suitable candidates for the vacant positions in the organisation. Thus, HR department of the company conducts a final round of interviews to select the best fit.

'Head hunters', a category of private agencies, cater mostly to the top management level recruitment needs. They handle executive search for organisations and usually charge high fees for their services.

Educational Institutions

During the placement season the educational institutions invite some of the best companies in their campus for recruitment. Organisations shortlist the institutions which can provide the kind of resources they are looking for and visit them during the placement season. Example, an organisation looking for management trainees visit the top ranking management schools. Thus, long-term relationships are built between organisations and educational institutions through this exercise of campus recruitment.

Interested Applicants

Candidates send their applications to the management either through post or by e-mail or in person and express their interest in employment with the company. If there is no suitable vacancy at that time, then applications are stored in it's data bank and use them whenever the need arises. Example, Johnson & Johnson has the concept of CV drop boxes. They maintain these boxes at all their offices for interested candidates to drop in their CVs. These CVs are collected, sorted out and stored in the CV databank on a monthly basis. Whenever there is a need for recruitment, the HR department checks its CV bank to find suitable candidates.

Other Sources

Sometimes, organisations consider non-traditional sources of recruitment while searching for certain types of applicants like, recruiting from the associations of the handicapped provide a highly motivated workforce and also help the organisation in building the image of a good corporate citizen.

Many organisations, use various methods and sources of recruitment and do not rely on any one particular method.

EVALUATION OF A RECRUITMENT PROGRAMME

The recruitment strategies, policies and objectives are evaluated from time to time to test their effectiveness to meet the organisational strategies, policies, and objectives. Likewise, the sources and methods of recruitment are also evaluated time to time to test their effectiveness and efficiency to match the recruitment policy, changing market and business needs.

The success of a recruitment programme may be judged based on a number of factors like :

- The number of applicants and successful placements
- The number of hirings and offers made
- The cost involved and the time taken for filling up the position

If a recruitment programme do not meet its objectives in terms of the number of successful placements, other factors like the number of applicants, the number of offers made and the number of hirings should be taken into consideration to understand the stage at which a discrepancy has occurred. For example, if the number of applicants is less, then probably there was a problem in attracting job-seekers. This may reflect a problem with the advertisement issued by the company, or a problem with the company's reputation. In case the number of applicants is high, and the offers made are low, it could mean that the company failed in attracting the right kind of candidates. Similarly, in case the number of successful placement is low, the problem may be that incumbents' expectations were not satisfied.

While evaluating a recruitment program the implications of cost and time is also analyzed, because, if needed the program may be revamped organisation on getting the required manpower but at a high cost.

MODEL QUESTIONS

1. What are the major factors that affects recruitment program?
2. What is recruitment policy?
3. Explain different sources of recruitment.
4. How the success of recruitment program is judged?
5. Explain the benefits of an employee referral programme.

CHAPTER

6

Selection

Concept

Selection is the next step after recruitment that involves a series of steps which help in evaluating the candidates. Most importantly, it the ability and inclination of the candidate to work in teams.

It is the process of ascertaining the qualifications, experience, skill, knowledge, etc. of an applicant with the purpose of determining his suitability for a job. The selection process starts with review of application form and ends with inducting the candidate into the organisation.

Selection process can have four possible outcomes. Out of these, two possible outcomes have a positive effect on the organisation, whereas the other two have a negative effect. The first positive outcome is selecting the right candidate.The second positive outcome is rejecting an unsuitable candidate, which can not perform successfully on the job.

The two negative outcomes are selecting an unsuitable candidate and rejecting the right candidate. Selecting an unsuitable candidate for the job is not useful for the organisation and may create problems. Because, organisations spend in their training and bears the cost of his non-performance. If he is replaced, the cost of separation and recruiting another candidate also add to the cost of selecting this unsuitable candidate. The second negative outcome is that if the right candidate is rejected, the organisation loses potential candidate who may be an asset to the organisation.

During the selection process, the candidates faces company representatives. While the candidate is being evaluated, he keeps assessing the company and its culture apart from the job. So, the representatives of the company should take care to project the company in the best possible way.

The Selection Process

The selection process in an organisation depends on the organisation's strategy and objectives.These objectives determine recruitment policy and the job design. The next step is 'competency modelling', that helps in identifying the knowledge, skill and attitude set that enables an individual to deliver the best performance in his job. Based on these, the selection criteria for a position can be identified.

Many organisations demand job applications, then conduct written tests and finally interview the candidates for selection.

The process of selection starts with a review of the applications. These applications can be either in a company specified format or in the format submitted by individual applicants. At this stage, the company checks the basic qualifications and experience of the candidates. Applicants who do not match the required basic criteria are rejected at this stage. Some companies conduct interview after the initial screening.

Steps in the Selection Process

The candidate called for the interview may face one-to-one interviews with representatives from the department concerned and some other departments which have to work in close coordination with the position. Finally, the candidate faces an interview with the manager concerned. Based on these interviews and the feedback received, the organisation decides whether to offer the applicant a job or not. This method of putting the candidate through a series of interviews is normally followed while selecting people for middle or senior level management positions.

During selection process, apart from evaluating his knowledge, attitude, emotional stability and value system and other things are also necessary to realize like - individual's inclination to learn, his interpersonal skills or his openness to suggestions etc. Because, these traits are more difficult to assess. So, it is the responsibility of the employer to assess these traits without annoying the applicant as these traits are essential for successful performance on the job.

SELECTION METHOD IDEALS

The selection methods are designed to ensure that they evaluate the candidates on the specified criteria. To ensure a more accurate prediction of the candidate's success in the future job, the selection methods should meet the generic standards of reliability, validity, generalisability, utility and legality.

Reliability

The selection method is considered reliable if it produces consistent results across different situations and times. If it produces different results when taken by the same individual at different times, the test is termed to be unreliable.

Validity

There are three general methods for determining the validity of a selection method.

Criterion validity

If there is a substantial correlation between the test scores and the job-performance scores, then the selection method would be considered valid.

Content validity

Content validity is the extent to which the content of a selection procedure is representative of important aspects of job performance.

Construct validity

Construct validity is the extent to which a selection method measures the degree of identifiable characteristics in the candidates.

Generalisability

It is defined as the degree to which its validity established in one context can be extended to the other primary contexts. These primary contexts can be different jobs or organisation, different samples of people and different time period.

Utility

The value provided by the selection methods enhances the effectiveness of an organisation. If the selection method is more reliable and valid then its utility is more. Still, there are external factors like the job market condition which may affect the utility of a selection method.

Legality

Legality is the basic standard that any selection method should satisfy. Every selection method should comply with the existing laws and legal provisions prevalent in the country.

APPLICATION FORMS

The application forms help in the initial screening of the applicants. These are designed to get information from the candidates regarding their qualifications, experience, the current responsibilities, the current salary and reference checks, which helps the recruiter to evaluate the applicants merit and this suitability for the job.

Some organisations use brief and concise application forms, while some others have elaborate ones.

Some of the items that usually appear on the application forms are:

1. **Personal Information :** It provides information about an applicant's name, date of birth of the candidate, gender, marital status, details of his family, occupations of other family members, annual income of the family, address, etc. These details help to form an idea of the socio-economic status of the applicant and his family background. Also, helps to assess his suitability in the organisation, in the job and in the team that he would be associated with.
2. **Educational Qualifications :** By this part the knowledge may be collected about period of study, the various courses taken and the subjects studied, the percentage of marks scored and the class or grade secured by him. This part of the application blank provides relevant information to assess an applicant's academic background.
3. **Work Experience :** This provides information about the applicant's previous jobs. List of previous employers, period of employment with each, tasks, activities and responsibilities handled and the salaries drawn are most usual details here. In some cases, reasons for leaving each of the organisations are also included. This helps the prospective employer to understand and evaluate the candidate's suitability to the job, his working habits and his competencies in relation to the job.
4. **Salary :** The salary of the applicant provides information of the salary drawn in his last job including benefits. It varies company to company, example a company has a low 'basic salary' but a high percentage of other components.

5. **Personality Items :** This aspect highlights his strengths and weaknesses, his professional goals - both long term and short term - and his hobbies and interests. This 'extra' information helps the employer to understand the personality of the applicant, which later helps in motivating him and improving his performance on the job.
6. **Reference checks :** In this section names and addresses of the individuals who can be contacted for a reference check of the applicant are included. This is one of the ways to check the credibility of the applicant.

Evaluation of Application Forms

Application forms are evaluated to analyze information provided by the applicants and select the suitable candidate. The following methods are used for evaluating the application forms.

Clinical Method

All the information provided/furnished by the applicant in the application form is analyzed and conclusions are drawn about the applicant's personality, and then his success in the job is predicted.

Weighted Method

In this method, certain points or weights are assigned to each item in the application form. The weighted application form differentiates the characteristics of successful and unsuccessful employees.

There are some of the questions that should not be asked in an application form as :

- That have no relevance in the context of the job.
- That evade the privacy of the applicant.
- That may lead to discrimination on any ground.
- That have adverse affect on the employment of women minorities, disabled or senior citizens.

SELECTION TESTS

There are different tests designed to evaluate different aspects of performance like intelligence, aptitude and attitude.

Intelligence Tests

It is the first standardized tests developed by psychologists and are the most widely used tests. It measures several factors of intelligence such as logical reasoning, analytical skills and general knowledge. It also measures a person's ability to classify things, identify relationships and derive analogies.

Aptitude Tests

It measures an individual's ability to learn a given job, after adequate training. They do not test the knowledge or proficiency possessed by the individual; instead they test his ability to learn or gain the required proficiency.

Achievement Tests

Achievement tests are also termed proficiency or knowledge tests. It measures the job-related proficiency and knowledge of the applicants.

Situational Tests

Situational tests are generally used in middle and senior level management selection to test the candidate's responses to real-life business situations. Situational tests include 'group discussions', 'in basket exercises' and 'simulated business games'.

In a 'group discussion', the members of the group interact on their own without any leader or moderator being specified. The initiative, leadership qualities, negotiating skills, communication skills and decision-making skills of the candidates can be assessed observing the group discussion.

The 'in-basket exercise' test the managerial and administrative skills of the candidate. In this candidate is exposed to a simulated office situation where he has to respond to letters, clear important documents, schedule his meetings, meet his colleagues and make some important business related decisions. In simulated business games, candidates play the role of a simulated character and are evaluated within a group.

Interest Tests

This test helps the companies to identify and understand the degree of interest a candidate has in a job. A candidate who looks for variety in his job may not be interested in doing a mechanical and monotonous job. These tests help in assessing an individual's genuine interest in a job and its profile.

Personality Tests

Personality test helps in understanding the basic job-related personality traits of an employee. Also, it helps in assessing an individual's value system, emotions, maturity and other personal characteristics.

INTERVIEWS

It forms a part of recruitment process. Because, it helps in assessing the candidate's profile and comparing it with the job profile for suitability and confirming the information provided in his application

The main disadvantage of an interview is individual biases based on gender, religion, race, nationality, caste, etc. often influence the decision of the interviewer. Some of the other reasons for bias may be the educational background, previous employer etc. of the candidate.

Preliminary Interview

Preliminary interviews are brief. Informal interviews can be conducted at any place by any person to secure information and to quickly evaluate the interviewee on the basis of appearance and quality of communication.

Selection Interview

The suitability of the candidate for the job is determined in these interviews. A selection interview can be of the following:

Formal and Structured Interview

In this interview the interviewer selects the questions to be asked and plans the event in advance. The main advantage of a structured interview is that there is no scope for subjectivity. The same questions are asked to all the candidates that help in better evaluation.

Unstructured Interview

An unstructured interview has no predetermined framework of questions and takes its own course depending on the responses of the candidate and the interest of the interviewer. The main advantage of this kind of interview is that the candidate remains comfortable during the course of the interview because the interaction proceeds naturally. The disadvantage is that such interviews become more subjective.

Stress Interview

The aim of this type of test is to test the applicant's ability to perform and deliver under stress. Interviewers put the interviewee under stress, repeatedly interrupting him, criticizing his answers, asking him unrelated questions or keeping quiet for long periods after the interviewee has finished speaking.

Panel Interview

Organisations prefer either a panel interview or a series of interviews where representatives from different departments meet and interview a candidate. This also reduces the subjectivity involved in the one-to-one interview.

Group Interview Method

This method is resorted to when the number of applicants is high and the time available for interviewing is short. This method is useful while recruiting for entry level and junior management levels. One advantage of this method is that the candidates can evaluate their own performance in comparison to the performance of others in the group.

Decision-Making Interview

After being evaluated by the experts in the core area of the job the candidate is finally interviewed by the HR manager and the department head. HR manager tries to find out the candidate's expectations regarding salary, allowances, benefits, promotions, and career opportunities. The departmental head and the HR manager together communicate their decision to the chairman of the interview board or the decision-making authority, who takes the final decision on selecting the candidate.

THE INTERVIEW PROCESS

The process of interview is long which passes through a series of activities and conducted simultaneously.

Preparation

The interviewer scan the application of the candidate to understand his background and experience to form an idea of the kind of questions that can be asked. The interviewer should follow these steps when preparing for the interview:

- Read the application of the candidate
- Determine the objectives of the interview.
- Determine the mode of evaluation.
- Plan one's time so as to allocate.
- Be prepared to interview.

Setting

It is the responsibility of the interviewer to make the candidate feel comfortable, relaxed and the atmosphere should be soothing. The performance of the candidate depends upon the internal atmosphere. Also, the interview room should be well lit and well ventilated. The interviewer must avoid attending phone calls, talking to colleagues, etc. during the interview, as they distract the candidate and only add to his tension.

Conduct of Interview

There are some basic guidelines to conduct a pleasant and fruitful interview as :

- Asking leading questions should be avoided by the interviewer because it gives the candidate a hint as to what answer is expected.
- The questions should not invade the privacy of the candidate.
- The interviewer should attentively listen to the answers of the candidate. In some panel interviews, it may happen that some of the panel members start discussing among themselves, while the candidate is answering another member's question. This shows disrespect to the panel member, to the candidate and also affects the validity of interview as a selection tool.
- The interviewer should mark relevant points during the conduct of the interview. These points help in evaluating the candidate at the end of the interview and can also be used as a future reference.

Closing an Interview

While closing the interview any awkward gestures and words must be avoided.

Evaluation

The evaluation of the candidate takes place when the candidate leaves the room. If the interviewer decides to evaluate all the candidates together at the end of the interviews, he may get influenced by the recency effect, which can distort the evaluation results.

Reference Checks

Before a candidate joins the organisation, the HR function with information provided in the application form of the candidate can confirm by the employer through these reference checks.

The individuals mentioned as referrals can be contacted through phone, official letters, e-mails or in person to establish the credentials of the candidate. Since this whole process takes some time to be completed, most of the organisations send offer to the candidate even before the reference checks are made.

Medical Examination

Many organisations have made physical medical examinations mandatory for hiring, Some companies which appoint candidates suffering from infections such as HIV positive, face problem. Because, people object to working with HIV infected people. Special privileges are given to handi-capped and under-privileged people in some organisations. So, they have their own medical standards for selection.

Induction

Once, an employee is selected and placed on an appropriate job the process of familarising him with the job and the organisation begins. This process is called induction or socialisation.

The purpose of orientation is to make the new incumbent feel at home and develop a sense of pride in the organisation and commitment to the job. Induction is the process of orientation.

According to Michael Armstrong. 'Orientation is the process of receiving and welcoming an employee when he first joins a company and give him the basic information he needs to settle down quickly and happily and start work.'

Socialisation

When a new employee joins an organisation, the human resource department helps him in learning the values of the organisation. Therefore, socialization is a process of learning and adaptation. In a broader sense, it is the sharing of the norms, values, beliefs and work culture of the organisation imparted to the new incumbent. This is a process which continues throughout the career of the employee which involves transfer, promotion or demotion.

Placement

A proper placement of an employee results in low employee turnover, low absenteeism and low accident rates.

Once, the candidate accepts the offer and joins, first inducted into the organisation and put on probation for a period ranging from six months to two years. After the initial probation period is over, the organisation decides the final placement based on the employee's performance during the period and his aptitude and interest. If the employee's performance is not satisfactory, the organisation may extend the probation period or ask the employee to quit. If the employee performs satisfactorily during this period, he is usually made a permanent employee.

MODEL QUESTIONS

1. Write notes on recruitment, selection, induction, socialization and placement.
2. Explain selection process of an organisation.
3. What is application form? What are it's advantages?
4. Interviews and its broad types.
5. Focus on interview process.

CHAPTER

7

Managing Careers

CONCEPT

A career can be defined as a sequence of positions, roles or jobs held by a person over a long period of time. It is not confined to one organisation.

Individual goals, aspirations and career opportunities change depending on various factors. For example, career goals are the future positions that an individual strives to reach as part of a career. Individual aspirations change due to changes in personal objectives, financial or other compulsions, new inclinations. Similarly, career opportunities change due to technological, socio-economic, political and organisational changes.

Career planning refers to the process by which an individual selects career goals and the path to these goals. The process whereby each employee personally plans career goals is known as individual career planning and the process whereby the organisation plans career goals for its employees is known as organisational career planning. Career management is the process of designing and implementing goals, plans and strategies that enable HR manager and professionals to satisfy workforce needs and allow the individuals to achieve their career objectives.

CONSTITUENTS OF A CAREER PLANNING PROGRAMME

There are some distinct elements or constituents of career planning as:

Assessment of Individual and Need Analysis

Assessment programmes evaluate employees on their abilities and competencies to perform in future positions. Organisation must guide each individual to make his own decisions regarding his career goal and career path. The HRD manager assist in this decision making process providing necessary information about the job, the future prospects, the career path and the employee himself. These employees are helped through workshops and assessment programs sponsored by the organisation. Workshops combine a number of career planning elements like self-assessment, communication of organisational opportunities and one-to-one counseling to ensure the career goals.

The need analysis identify the training and development exercises that help the individual to meet his career plans as well as organisational objectives. There are many reasons due to which an employee opt a particular occupation or organisation like financial needs, family background, inadequate knowledge and improper guidance.

Purpose of need analysis:

- to determine his knowledge, skills, competencies and attitudes;
- to identify the areas that need training inputs;
- to understand the career aspirations of the employee.
- to communicate the results of the analysis.

Opportunity Analysis

The information to the employees about career advancement, specific job vacancies and technological changes helps them to analyze their prospects.

It gives greater flexibility and job enrichment to the employee as he is allowed to switch jobs wherein he gets an opportunity to learn new things. It is better than a traditional path because a traditional career path is based on the organisation's past needs for human resources.

Alignment of Opportunity

The organisation, and the HR function, helps the employee to make this alignment. As, the HR function has a formalised system of tracking and recording career moves across the organisation.

Career Counselling

The supervisor, along with the HR department, counsel the employee regarding his aspirations, competencies and the available opportunities. In career counselling sessions, employees normally seek answers to questions like:

- Why do I seek a career?
- What are my actual needs, prospects and the opportunities available ?
- What are the requirements of the jobs ?
- What training I require if I choose to pursue ?

Career Planning Benefits to an Organisation

The well-planned and career planning programmes are beneficial for employees as well as the organisation. It enables an organisation to manage its human resources better and provide the following positive results:

Future Availability of Resources

Career planning and development helps in meeting the resource requirement for future. And human resource planning determines the changing resource requirements of an organisation.

Attracting and Retaining Talents

A good career planning becomes more essential and responsibilities increases as better talents are attracted and retained.

Growth Opportunities

Career planning helps in maintaining the growth opportunities of employees of different categories at each level in the organisation.

Ensures Realistic Goal

Career counselling is an integral part of career management that helps employees to set realistic and achievable goals for employees. A good career development programme helps in meeting the expectations of the employees.

Career Planning Benefits to an Individual

Career planning offers the following benefits to employees:

(*i*) It enables him to choose a career.

(*ii*) It helps the employee to identify his own strengths and weaknesses and to achieve career objective that suits his lifestyle, preferences, self-development plans.

(*iii*) It helps the employee to have a better knowledge of the career opportunities and plan his career in a long term prospective.

(*iv*) It provides him an opportunity to change his career plans.

ISSUES IN CAREER PLANNING

Career Development in Unison

The career development in unison or dual-career planning is important when both the husband and wife are employed in the same organisation, then emphasis must be given on there career development in unison.

Low Ceiling Careers

In an organisation for some jobs there are little possibility for advancement in terms of career. Still, employees seek some form of career progression.

Declining Career Opportunities

In some jobs there are declining career opportunities due to technological economic changes. For example, career opportunities for statisticians have come down due to a high degree of computerization.

Issues of Work-family

Most of the employees face some constraints in pursuit of their career objective like - elderly parents, school-going kids, a sick relative or family member etc.

Career Stages

The employees move through different career stages and their career needs change when they move from one stage to another.

Restructuring

The demands and expectations of a fast changing economy force organisations to restructure and reorganize themselves.

Career Saturation

The employees reach a saturation point in their career if they feel nothing else left to achieve. Example - stress, lack of knowledge, lack of opportunities, lack of motivation can lead to a career saturation.

CAREER DEVELOPMENT

It is a series of stages by which an individual passes as – the first one life-cycle model, that is based on different stages and states an individual grows through these stages in his career. Then comes organisational-based model which explains that careers progress through different stages through which some activities are attached to. Another one is direction-pattern model that states different perspectives of employees, their careers and their plans to progress. For example, when an employee decides to continue in the same job or occupation for life, it is called a linear approach. Similarly, another employee consider to shift another job for various reasons which is called a spiral approach.

Exploration Stage

At this stage, the individuals try to identify their inclination towards different kinds of work considering their values, interests, work preferences, careers and occupations. Then, on the basis of their own analysis, they start pursuing the required education or training. Usually, the new employee tries to align the job and his own aptitude. During induction and orientation program he is prepared to take on new tasks and roles in the organisation with the help and direction of colleagues.

Settlement Stage

In this stage, an individual tries to identify his job and wants desirable life styles. Also, thinks to take more responsibility, makes independent contributions to the organisation.

Maintenance and Utilisation Stage

At this stage, an individual tries to refresh his experiences and also the organisational policies. Also, understands that how an organisation conducts its business and how the economy affects it's business.

Disengagement Stage

At this stage, an individual choose to change their career tracks or occupations. In some cases, they may even decide to quit their career and devote their time to pursue their family life, hobbies etc.

CAREER OBJECTIVES AND THE CAREER PATH

The career path of an employee passes through different stages to achieve final career objectives. Some of them are internal like transfers, promotions,seperations etc. whereas some are external as a change in the organisation occupation.

Promotion

Promotion refers to a move of an employee in the organisation to another job which has greater importance, higher challenges and usually higher pay. It is based on performance in the current position, ability to take up a higher position and in some cases, the seniority of the employee. Employee experience depends on their abilities and responsibilities and also authority and status.

Types of promotions : merit-based, seniority based, seniority and merit based.

Merit based promotions are awarded to those employees who show excellent performance throughout in their job.

Seniority based promotions are given to employees who have been loyal to the organisation for the long years and have served at a particular level in the organisation. These promotions are given irrespective of the performance or contribution of the employee.

Seniority and merit based promotions for this type of promotions, individuals have to work for long years with the organisation and also deliver good performance and contribution consistently.

There is one more classification of promotions that is *time-bound and vacancy-based.*

In the *time-bound promotions*, employees are promoted after a fixed tenure at a particular level. This is similar to seniority-based promotions.

Vacancy-based promotions are similar to seniority and merit based promotions. Employees are judged based on their performance and contribution at the same level and the best one from the lot is promoted to the vacant position at the next level.

Purpose of Promotion

- To give recognition to job well done by an employee during his service years.
- To retain and reward employees for their long years of service to the organisation.

Principles of Promotion

If, carefully handled promotions lead to employee satisfaction and motivation. And if, mishandled it results in frustration and culminates in a high rate of labor turnover. The important point to note are:

- The management must make it clear whether to fill up higher positions by internal promotions or recruit people from outside.
- The criteria for promotion must be based fair and based on appraisal.
- Unsuccessful candidates must be treated sympathetically.

Transfer

It is a move to a job within the company which has round about equal importance, status and compensation.

Types of transfer - employee initiated transfers, company initiated transfers, public initiated transfers.

Employee initiated transfers or personal transfers are primarily in the interest of the employee, to match his needs.

Company initiated transfers are primary in the interest of the company to cater to the changing demands and requirements of the company.

Public initiated transfers are initiated by the government/politicians for various reasons like disciplinary action or special assignments.

Purpose of Transfer

(*i*) *Employee needs* - to maintain employee turnover, promotions, demotions, terminations may result in job vacancies which may be filled up through transfer.

(*ii*) *Organisational needs* - to maintain balance in the manpower may result in employee transfer.

Principles of Transfer

- A transfer is regarded as a reselection.
- The need for a transfer is explained.
- Unsatisfactory employees are not transferred to other departments.
- Requests by employees are fully investigated
- No employee is transferred to another district against his will.
- An employee transferred to another district is given financial assistance from the company to cover removing costs, legal fees, refurnishing etc.

Seperations

Seperation means cessation of service of agreement with the organisation for one or other reason. The employee may be separated from the payroll of accompany as a result of resignation.

An employee resigns on securing a better job elsewhere. In the case of female, when marries and quit on personal reasons or when suffers from ill-helath. It refers to the termination of employment at the condition of employees.

Discharge and Dismissal

The dismissal or discharge means the termination of employment initiated by the employer. The reasons to the dismissal of an employee are :

- Excessive absenteeism.
- Serious misconduct
- False statement of the qualification at the time of employment
- Theft of company's property.

Suspension : It refers to the termination of the services of the employee because of the replacement of labour by machines or the closure of a department due to continuing lack of demand for the products manufactured in that particular department of the organisation. If the plant is closed the management and the employees leaves the organisation permanently.

Suspension differs from lay off. In lay offs the employees continues to be in the employment of the organisation and is sure to be recalled after the end of the period of it. Whereas, in suspension the employee is to leave permanently.

Suspension differs from dismissal as well. The dismissal involves the termination of the services of one or two employees. An employee may be dismissed because of their own fault. Suspension is forced on both the employer and his employees. Also, it involves the termination of the services of many employees.

Layoff

A lay-off means a temporary separation of the employee from the employer. It may be for a definite period after that the employee may be recalled by the employer for the duty. Sometime it may extend to any length of time. If the employees are laid-off at the decision of the employer they have to be paid compensation for the period they are laid off. The compensation must be equal to half the normal wages the employee earned if they had not been laid-off.

The basis for the lay-off may be merit or seniority. If merit is the basis, the employees with unsatisfactory performance are laid off first. In the unionized company competence as the basis for lay off is not possible. In such companies, the seniority determines who should be first laid off. Without any notice the employees whose service tenure is lesser are first laid off and whose service tenure is too long are retained as long as the conditions permit. After the lay off the management recalls the key employees first.

SELF-DEVELOPMENT

An individual self-development passes through different stages. In the first step the individual realise his strengths, weaknesses, competencies and aspirations. Then in the next step makes evaluation of the opportunities and the changing market trends. Afterwards in the third step decision is taken after comparison of the factors in the first two steps. Then comes the fourth step, where the Individual avails suitable opportunity in support of his contacts. Then in the final step the individual sets out his career path or changes his career path. And in the last step makes evaluation of the changing opportunities aspirations and competencies.

Self-assessment

The beginning of a career planning for self-development starts with an analysis of one's personality, skill, knowledge, values and interests. The ability to learn and be a self-starter should also be considered while evaluating an individual's capabilities.

Evaluation of Opportunities

The individuals at this stage make the best use of the available opportunities, make search for the right contacts, who can help them to get the desired job.

Career and Venture

At this stage, the individual assesses the offers made to him to start his career and venture into the job that suits him the best. He adapts a new role, a new organisation and a new occupation.

Regular Assessment

Once, the individual enters the new job and settles down, he goes on assessing the changing trends and opportunities to make the best use of the available opportunities.

Evaluation of Competencies

At this stage, he assesses whether to be suitable for a new assignment or not.

SUCCESSION PLANNING

It helps the organisation to identify specific individuals to fill the future vacancies in key positions. It also helps to have an overview of the present Job holder and the prospective replacements. An efficient and succession planning incorporates the following constituents:

Long-term Perspective

The development of the employees must match the high standards to ensure the availability of replacement, when the need arises.

Organisational Need Perspective

In case an organisation needs some fresh or external talent, the employees of the organisation should be in a position to accept it as natural and justified decision.

Continuity

The succession planning is not an annual event. Every manager strives to develop at least one candidate as a potential replacement.

Turnover Management

The suitable action plans are developed to generate turnovers and avoid positions becoming blocked.

MODEL QUESTIONS

1. Focus on different elements of a career planning.
2. What are the benefits of a carrier planning to an individual?
3. What are the issues in career planning?
4. Discuss career development cycle.
5. Write notes on promotion, transfer and separation.
6. Explain the stages of self development.

CHAPTER

8 Performance Appraisal

CONCEPT

The performance of an organisation is managed monitoring the performance of the individual employees in the organisation. So, the successful performance of an organisation is a culmination of individual performances and contributions.

Performance appraisal can be defined as the process of evaluating the performance of an employee and communicating the results of evaluation to him for the purpose of rewarding or developing the employee.

The term 'performance' appraisal is concerned with the process of rating an employee's worth to an organisation, with a view to increase it. So, most of the performance appraisal systems are linked to rewards systems as well as employee development systems. It is also important that the appraisal system matches the organisational culture. For example, a 360 degree feedback systems, would not deliver results if it is implemented in a traditional organisation which has rigid hierarchies.

Although, performance appraisal and potential evaluation are used synonymously, but performance appraisal is a wider term than potential evaluation. The potential evaluation evaluates the different traits of the employee by comparing the qualitative factors such as nature of the individual, physical and mental ability etc. Whereas performance appraisal evaluates the performance of an employee by comparing the quantitative factors such as quantity of output and rejected output, standard of work etc.

According to Flippo: "Performance appraisal is a systematic, periodic and so far as humanly possible and impartial rating of an employee's excellence in matters pertaining to his present job and to his potentialities for a better job."

Whereas, according to Flippo "Potential evaluation attempts to systematic,periodic and so far as humanly possible, an impartial rating of an employee's excellence in matters pertaining to his present job and to his potentialities for a job."

Purposes of Performance Appraisal

- to improve job performance and identify the potentialities for other work.
- To identify the need and areas for further training of the employees.
- To assist in determining promotion and transfer policies.
- To reduce the grievances among the employees
- To make the compensation plans more scientific and rational.
- To help in proper placement of the workers after the completion of their training.
- To facilitate research in personnel management.
- To develop positive relations in between superior and subordinate.

Q. What is appraisal and how it is to be implemented ?

- it is a two-way discussion between the appraiser and the appraisee.

- It is an pen document that both appraiser and the appraisee agrees and sign.
- It is a plan for future.
- It is a constructive criticism of the performance and personality of the appraisee in the immediate past.
- It's meeting without emotions are being involved.

THE APPRAISAL PROCESS

1. The first step in the appraisal process is to find out the standards of performance based on the organisation objectives and the job description. It is easier to evaluate performance, if goals and standards are specific and quantifiable.
2. The second step in the appraisal process is the measurement of employee performance against pre-determined goals and standards.
3. The third step is the actual process of measurement. Performance appraisal is a continuous process and the feedback should be given to the employee at regular intervals. This helps the employees to track their performance and grooms them for higher responsibilities.
4. The fourth step is communicating the results of appraisal to the employee concerned. It is the responsibility of the manager to make the employee feel comfortable with the whole process.
5. The final step is to put into effective use. Whatever may be the organisational policy, the document of appraisal has to be put into use effectively and immediately to ensure a better performance during the next appraisal period.

Many organisations do not get acceptance and support from their employees for their performance appraisal system because of lack of commitment of the top management.

Limitations

Performance appraisal may not yield the desired results because of the following deficiencies :

- if the factors included in the assessment are irrelevant, the result of potential evaluation is not accurate.
- different qualities to be evaluated may not be given proper weightage in certain cases.
- some of the factors are highly subjective like initiative and personality of the employees so that actual evaluation may not be on scientific lines.
- supervisor often do not have critical ability in assessing the staff. Sometimes, they are guided by their personal emotions and likes. So, the evaluation are likely to be biased.

Effective Appraisal System

An appraisal system to be effective it needs to be based on the following elements :

- the performance appraisal should be performance based, uniform and non variable, fair, just and equitable. It should be ensured that the appraisers are honest, rational and objective in their approach, judgement and behavioral operation.
- Periodic goal setting.
- Periodic or annual assessment of performance in terms of such goals –
  - (*a*) identifying facilitating and inhabitating factors in relation to the achievement of goals.
  - (*b*) Development of action plans for overcoming inhabitating factors and strengthening the facilitating factors.
- the results of performance appraisal must be immediately communicated to the employees especially

when they are negative so that they may try to improve their performance and also they may be able to know where do they stand.

- Periodic review of behavior which contributes to management effectiveness.
- Identification of development needs.

THE APPRAISERS

The employee in coordination with his supervisor, decides the performance objectives and standards. After the appraisal period the appraiser offers his opinion to the employee. Then employee on the basis of the opinion of appraiser assesses his own performance, in comparison to the pre-determined objective.

In 360 degree feedback system, the peers of the employee, suppliers, customers and even his subordinates helps in the identification of problem areas.

Self-Appraisal

The employee on the basis of his strength and weaknesses evaluates his performance and easily identifies the problem areas that need training and development.

Supervisors

The supervisor has a very important role in the appraisal of his subordinates. Many of them fear to take the exercise, as they do not want to spoil their relationship with the employee.

Peers

Peer appraisal is used to assess the communication and interpersonal skills of the employee, which can affect the team performance.

Customer/Clients

In service organisation like banks and hotels, customer feedback is most important tool in evaluating performance of the employee. In manufacturing organisation, the internal customer evaluates the performance of the employee.

Subordinates

The subordinate evaluates the performance of his supervisor which is prevailing fast in most of the organisations. Example, in 360 degree feedback system, the appraisal by subordinates is being adopted by many organisations.

PERFORMANCE APPRAISAL METHODS

The different appraisal methods used by the organisations are:

1. Management by objectives or goal-setting	Traditional Methods
2. Graphic rating scale	
3. Work standards approach	
4. Essay appraisal	
5. Critical incident method	
6. Forced choice rating method	
7. Point allocation method	
8. Ranking methods	
9. Checklist	
10. Behaviorally anchored rating scale (BARS)	Modern Methods
11. 360 degree performance appraisal	
12. Team appraisals	
13. Balanced scorecard method	

Management by Objectives (MBO)

Management by objectives is also called goal-setting approach. It is more commonly used for managers and professionals. For successful implementation of MBO, the followings are required:

- measurable goals
- suitable and motivated employees
- regular feedback
- evaluation of performance and corrective action

Graphic Rating Method

This method rates the employee on factors such as quantity and quality of work, job knowledge, dependability, punctuality, attendance etc. Graphic rating scale includes numerical ranges as well as written descriptions.

There are two disadvantages of this method. One disadvantage is that the important ones may get missed out and the irrelevant ones may get included. The second disadvantage is that different people may interpret the written descriptions in different ways.

Work Standards Approach

This method of appraisal is suitable in a manufacturing scenario, where the goals are predetermined work standard. The advantage of this approach is that the goals are measurable. The disadvantage is that the work standards for different job categories cannot be compared.

Essay Appraisal

In the Essay Appraisal method, questions or guidelines are provided to the appraiser, based on that he analyses and describes the employee's performance. If the appraiser concentrates on a single aspect or misses out an important aspect of performance the appraisal will be incomplete or inadequate. Similarly, it is difficult to compare the performance of two employees, based on the descriptions of their performance provided by different supervisors. The advantage of this system is that the appraiser can express his views on the employee's performance, without any constraints.

Critical Incident Method

In this method the appraiser makes a record of all the critical incidents that reflect the performance or behavior of the employee during the appraisal period. At the end of the appraisal period, this record forms the basis for the evaluation of performance of the employee. This method of appraisal is rarely used because of the ambiguity involved and the effort required in recording the incidents.

Forced Choice Rating Method

In this method, the appraiser assign ranks to different attributes of the employee. Once, the employee attributes are ranked, the human resource department applies weights and arrives at a score which is the final appraisal score.

Point Allocation Method

In this method of appraisal, the appraiser assigns different points to different members in his team based on their performance during the appraisal period. The best performer gets the highest score and the last one in the team gets the least score. One disadvantage is that an appraiser can allocate equal points to everyone in the group, ignoring the differences in their performance.Another disadvantage is that the difference in point allocation may not reflect the differences in performances across groups

Ranking Methods

There are three commonly used methods of ranking- as alternation, paired comparison and forced distribution. The first two methods are used when there are only a few employees to be ranked, whereas forced distribution method is used in large companies like GE, Microsoft and Wipro, where thousands of employees are to be ranked.

In the first method, alternation, the appraiser ranks all his employees based on their performance and contributions to the organisation. In the paired comparison method, the appraiser ranks the employees, based on paired comparison. The forced distribution method is very popular method of performance appraisal in big organisations. In this method the employees are categorized as 'Top', 'Standard' and 'Bottom' and placed under a forced-distribution.

Checklist

In this method, weights are attached to each of the questions based on which the final appraisal score of the employee is calculated. Major disadvantage is that different checklist is designed for different jobs that may make the whole exercise cumbersome and complex.

Behaviourally Anchored Rating Scale (BARS)

The BARS concentrates on the behavioral traits instead of his actual performance.

There are three steps in implementing BARS system. They are:

1. Determination of different job aspects by the manager and the employee.
2. Determination of the parameters to be used and grouping of traits for each scale parameters, based on consensus.
3. Identification of different traits by the manager and the employee for each job dimension.

The main advantage of BARS is that both the manager and the employees are actively involved in the appraisal process. One drawback of this system is it is inconvenient and takes much time in development.

360 Degree Performance Appraisal

In this ystem, the employee's performance is evaluated by the peers, customers, suppliers and subordinates of the employee, who are directly affected by his behavior and performance, apart from the boss.It is held annually and conducted in the following ways.

- Self appraisal
- Subordinate
- HOD's/Functional Head
- Outside agencies like customers,venders,dealers,govt agencies.

- By the superiors, while giving ratings all the above levels of BARS must be submitted to him before he gives his own ratings
- Appraisal committee represented by Sr. Managers.

Team Appraisals

In the team appraisal method, the individual team members evaluate their colleagues in the team and provide feedback. This helps in coordinating individual efforts and taking the group performance to higher levels.

Balanced Score-card

This method while measuring performance concentrates the efforts of people to achieve organisational goals. The assigning of responsibilities to individuals and tracking for achievement of objectives is called HR score-card. The HR score-card seeks to give online feedback to the employees as to how they are faring. In some cases, their salaries are linked to their performance. It is a part of balanced score-card.

Many top Indian companies such as Infosys, i2 Technologies, Godrej Consumer Products, GTL, ITC Ltd. and Mahindra & Mahindra are using this method of performance management.

THE APPRAISAL INTERVIEW

In modern organisations the employee himself evaluates his own performance on various factors mentioned in the appraisal form and assesses his strengths and weaknesses. This helps him to identify the areas that need training or development inputs.

Challenges of Appraisal Interview

The atmosphere in an appraisal interview is usually comfortable, as the appraisee is apprehensive in receiving any negative feedback, and the appraiser is cautios of giving such feedback. So, Some of the main challenges of an appraisal interview are:

The Organisation Culture

If, there is absence of right kind of organisational culture then it leads to an ineffective process of performance appraisal.

Boss-employee Relationship

The general relationship between the employee and his boss is the biggest factor of the interview.

The Maturity Level of the Individuals

If the supervisor gives a feedback saying that the employee needs to improve in a few areas, an immature or unprofessional individual may react in a defensive way, leading to unpleasantness.

A Cautious Appraiser

The appraiser, with a view to maintain a cordial relationship with appraise, may restrain to give any negative or constructive feedback. This makes the whole exercise futile.

A Partial Appraiser

Often, the appraiser may be partial or against the appraisee for various reasons. This may lead to negative feedback, which renders the exercise futile.

Lack of Experience

Lack of experience to the process of performance appraisal may result ineffective which may not benefit the individual or the organisation.

DRAWBACKS IN PERFORMANCE APPRAISAL

Some of the constituents that affect the appraisal process at an individual level are:

Culture : The culture of the organisation or the country influence the appraiser to rate the appraise in a particular way.

Stereotyping : It involves judging someone based on the group he belongs to and the appraiser's perception of the group. For example, An appraiser who believes that women may be good managers so rate his female appraisees better than his male appraisees.

Halo effect : The appraiser/rater commits an error in evaluating the performance of the appraisee on the basis of a single trait like – appearance, punctuality, co-operativeness etc. A certain positive trait of a person may ignore all other characteristics that have to be considered while evaluating performance.

Leniency effect : The situation where the appraiser gives high ratings and only positive feedback to the appraisee, irrespective of his actual performance. The main reason for leniency may be the appraiser's desire to maintain a cordial relationship with the appraisee.

Stringency effect : An appraiser who feels that the rules and standards of the organisation are not strict enough, tries to be strict in rating his appraisees.

Regency effect : An employee, who has performed well for the preceding nine months but failed to maintain the same level of performance in the last three months preceding the appraisal, may get the same rating as, someone who performed well only in the last 2-3 months of the appraisal period. This is due to the recency effect.

Primacy effect : The performance of the appraisee at the beginning of the appraisal period dominates the evaluation.

Central tendency effect : It is the tendency of the appraiser to rate most of the appraisee in the middle of the performance.

Perceptual set : When a perceived low performer exceeds the expectations of his appraiser, his performance is judged higher than it deserves to be may distort the perception and judgment of actual performance.

USES OF PERFORMANCE APPRAISAL

Apart from evaluating the performance of the employees for rewards/punishments a good performance appraisal system has many other uses. Some of these are listed below:

- Training and development needs of the employees can be determined.
- The performance appraisal system forms the basis for compensation management transfers, promotions and other career planning activities.
- It helps in improving organisation effectiveness and thereby improving the individual performances of the employees.
- It helps in succession planning in the organisation to evaluate human resources of the firm based on the competency, skill set and potential of the workforce.
- It helps in evaluating and auditing the existing plans, processes and systems in the organisation.
- It helps in cross-functional transfers and job enrichment exercises etc., based on inputs from the appraisal system.

MODEL QUESTIONS

1. Explain performance appraisal with its objectives.
2. Explain different methods of appraisals.
3. Write short notes on behaviourally anchored rating scale (BARS), 360 degree performance appraisal, team appraisals and balanced scorecard method.
4. Explain the drawbacks in performance appraisal system.
5. Focus on appraisal interview.

CHAPTER

9 Compensation Management

CONCEPT

The compensation for employee should be designed and implemented properly as it one of the major determinants of employee satisfaction in an organisation. A good compensation system attract and retain and motivate employees to perform their best.

Job evaluation helps to determine the relative worth of a job in an organisation in a systematic, consistent and accurate manner. It also helps in estimating the basic pay for each job in accordance with the importance of the job in the organisational hierarchy. Once the basic pay is determined, the rewards, incentives and benefits attached with the pay, position and performance also determined.

It is a systematic process of analysing and evaluating jobs to determine the relative worth of each job in an organisation. Apart from job evaluation, the various factors that determine the compensation system are the size and structure of the organisation,the strength of employee unions and above all, the profitability of the company.

Objectives

The objectives of compensation management are:

- to determine the relative worth of different jobs.
- to manage internal and external consistency.

- to determine the position and place of a job in the organisational hierarchy and maintain accurate data relating to job description.
- to clarify the responsibility and authority associated and to ensure employee satisfaction.
- to avoid discrimination of any kind in wage administration.

Principles of Job Evaluation

The principles of job evaluation are as follows.

(*a*) The evaluation programme should be explained to the employee.

(*b*) The job dimensions must be properly selected and properly defined

(*c*) The employee must be involved in the evaluation program.

(*d*) The market factors must be considered while evaluating jobs.

PROCESS OF JOB EVALUATION

The steps involved in a job evaluation exercise are as

Job Analysis – It helps in understanding the tasks and responsibilities associated with a job and the competency set required to perform the tasks and fulfil the responsibilities.

- *Job Description and Job Specification* – Job description is a compilation of the tasks, duties responsibilities associated with each job in the organisation. Job specification is a compilation of the knowledge, skills and attitudes required to perform each job successfully.
- *Selection of Job dimensions* – The different factors which is the basis for evaluating each must be determined. Once, the dimensions are settled monetary values are attached to each of these jobs after proper assessment.

- *Classification of jobs* – Jobs are classified in sequential order on the basis of the monetary values attached to them.
- *Implementation of the evaluation* – The employees should be educated about the programme to make them understand the basis and the procedure of job evaluation.
- *Maintenance* – The results of job evaluation are updated and modified time to time to match the changing organisational needs and job profiles.

Techniques of Job Evaluation

There are two techniques like quantitative and non-quantitative techniques which are used to compare jobs in an organisation.

QUANTITATIVE TECHNIQUE

Point Rating Method

This is a method where a quantitative point scale is developed to evaluate the job. Example, all the managerial jobs may be evaluated on one scale, all the operational jobs on another and all the clerical jobs, perhaps on a third one. The number of scale to be used and other aspects of implementation determine job evaluation.

1. *Determine the job factors or compensable factors :* These characteristics are deemed important by the organisation and which are present in all the jobs to be evaluated.
2. *Determine the job sub-factors :* These are subdivided into 'sub factors', which are essential/specific to the job being evaluated due to their broad meaning. Example, engineering knowledge may be a job factor while dexterity may be a sub factor for the job of a maintenance engineer.

3. *Define the degree statements or profile statements :* Degree statements describe the specific requirements of each sub factor. There are normally up to five degrees associated with each sub factor.
4. *Assign points to factors, sub-factors and degrees :* On the basis of the importance of each factor, sub-factor and degree in the job, points are assigned to them. Example "if experience" is critical to a job, degree I may be 20 points degree II may be 40 points, degree III – 60 points, degree IV – 80 points and degree V – 100 points. The maximum points that can be allotted to each job are fixed and these points are distributed across different job factors.
5. *Preparation of a chart :* A chart is prepared to give weight to factors and sub-factors.
6. *Applying the point system :* The point helps in determining the pay scale of each job. After the points for each job are finalized, jobs are ranked based on their points.

ADVANTAGES

- The system is accurate and dependable.
- It can be used for a long time, with timely updates.

DISADVANTAGES

- It is a complex and time-taking assignment.
- This method involves high costs and a lot of clerical work.

Factor Comparison Method

The steps for factor comparison are—

(*a*) The first step is to determine and define the specific factors across different jobs.

(*b*) The second step is to identify the key jobs or benchmark jobs, which are well known and have an established pay rate in the organisation.

(c) The factors in each key jobs are compared with the benchmark and ranked, based on their relative importance.

(d) The factors are then assigned monetary.

(e) The remaining jobs in the organisation are then evaluated based on the evaluation of key jobs/ benchmark jobs.

ADVANTAGES

- It is an analytical, objective, logical and quantitative method.
- It is easy to explain to supervisors, employees and unions.

DISADVANTAGES

- It is very cumbersome and complex method.
- In case of a mismatch between the factor comparison and factor ranking method, the exercise has to be started from the beginning.

Decision Band Method

This method (DBM) has been used successfully in public and private organisations throughout the world for over 25 years, but it is not a conventional method of job evaluation.

The main idea of DBM is that the value of a job depends on its decision-making requirements. Decision-making is a logical and equitable basis for comparing jobs, because all jobs require the holder of the job to make decisions of some kind in order to perform their jobs. The DBM distinguishes six level of decision making ranging from the most far reaching decision to the simplest decisions.

Non-Quantitative Techniques

There are two types of non quantitative techniques like ranking and job grading methods.

Ranking

Although it is one of the simplest and oldest job evaluation methods still it is rarely used because this method does not have an objective and concrete basis of evaluation. Jobs in an organisation are assessed based on the knowledge, skills, effort and other job dimensions associated with each job.

The techniques for ranking used in the process of job evaluation are :

(*a*) **Relative ranking :** As, it is difficult to rank all the jobs at a time so relative ranking method is adopted. A key or representative job is identified and its worth is determined. Then, the relative importance of each job in comparison with the key representative job is determined & then ranked.

(*b*) **Paried comparison :** Each job is compared with other job in the organisation. After the comparison in pairs the jobs are ranked.

(*c*) **Single factor ranking :** The single most important factor of a job is identified and compared with a single most important factor of other jobs.

Once the ranking of the jobs is complete, monetary value is attached to each job.

ADVANTAGES

- This method of evaluation is very simple and appropriate.
- This system is a quick and inexpensive method of job evaluation.

DISADVANTAGES

- No definite standard is used for ranking so it is not suitable for large organisations.
- Job specification and employee specification are not considered in evaluation.

Job Grading

The jobs are classified and graded based on their significance & worth to the organisation. Grades are formulated on the basis of nature of tasks and responsibilities of the jobs. A single grade is assigned to the different jobs across the company at the same level. For example, a grade may comprise jobs like financial Accountants, cost Accountants, and Management Accountants. The steps in job grading are—

(*a*) to analyze the organisational structure and its chief characteristics. For example, determining whether the organisation is a functional or a matrix organisation structure.

(*b*) to definine the job grades as Grade I, Grade II and so on based on the job dimensions and the organisation structure.

(*c*) to classify the jobs of the organisation under different grades.

ADVANTAGES

- It is simple and inexpensive technique and easy to understand, once the grade definition and job classification exercise is complete.
- Any changed job or a new job can be easily evaluated after the grades are established.

DISADVANTAGES

- It is cumbersome method as the grades cover different jobs from different functions. For example, a grade that cover the job of a human resources officer also cover the job of a finance officer.

ADVANTAGES OF JOB EVALUATION

(*a*) It facilitates the entry of new jobs.

(*b*) It is a logical and objective method of ranking and grading jobs.

(*c*) It helps to prevent and remove discrepancies in the wage structure.

(*d*) It can explain logically any issue relating to wage differentials.

(*e*) The information collected for job evaluation can be used for decisions related to selection, transfer and promotion of employees.

LIMITATIONS OF JOB EVALUATION

(*a*) It reduces rigidity into the pay system.

(*b*) Job evaluation can give rise to employee grievances if not properly formulated or implemented.

(*c*) It reduces opportunities for managers to take decision.

(*d*) It takes a long time to implement, also may involve some formalization of rules.

Concept of Wage and Salary Administration

The wage and salary are the foundation of employee pay structure, and total compensation is calculated after these are fixed. It is a system of compensating employees in a fair manner and maintaining the principle of equity and expectancy.

Administering Principles for Compensation

The principles governing the administration are:

(*a*) to match employee expectations.

(*b*) to equity in the distribution of wages and salaries.

(*c*) to competitiveness in the wage market.

(*d*) to reinforcing positive employee behaviour and contribution to the organisation.

(*e*) to maintain good industrial relations and harmony with respect to compensation.

Purpose of Wage and Salary Administration

The basic purpose of a salary compensation administration in an organisation is to satisfy employees' needs to motivate and retain them.

(*a*) *Attracting talented resources* – A good competitive compensation system helps in attracting good talent from the job market. A competitive salary is useful especially when there is a high demand for a particular trade or skill.

(*b*) *Retaining and motivating employees* – A fair and rewarding compensation helps in retaining employees and motivating them to perform better.

(*c*) *Financial management* – A rational compensation system helps the management to reduce its costs in terms of employee turnover and ensures better return on investment.

(*d*) *Legal requirements* – an organisation having branches in many countries also needs to comply with the different laws in different part of the world. For example, the minimum wage in one country may be different from the minimum wage in another.

Concepts of Different Wages

Over the centuries the concept of wages differ. Different types of wages are as:

Minimum Wage

It is the amount of remuneration, either the minimum-piece rate or minimum-time rate to enable an average worker to fulfill all his obligations. It is fixed by the government and enforced by the law with respect to all the scheduled employments. It is revised at least once in five years based on the consumer price index. The current minimum wage in India's is Rs. 50 per day to all the workers in scheduled employment. It is applicable to workers across the country and is governed by the Minimum wage Act, 1948.

"Minimum wages" are fixed on different norms:

(*i*) A minimum food requirement should be calculated on the basis of net intake of calories.

(*ii*) The clothing requirements should be estimated as per capita consumption of 18 yards per annum.

(*iii*) In respect of housing, the rent should be taken into consideration in fixing the minimum wage.

(*iii*) Fuel, lighting and other miscellaneous items of expenditure should constitute 20 per cent of the total minimum wage.

(*iv*) Children's education, medical requirements, minimum recreation including festivals etc., should constitute 25 per cent.

Fair Wage

The workers receive equal fair wages for work of equal skill, difficulty or unpleasantness. The recommendations of the committee regarding fair wage are:

- The basis of fair wage is the minimum wage.
- Fair wage should be related to the productivity of the labour and should reflect the level of national income.
- It should match the prevailing rates of wages.

Living Wage

It is a wage which provide the certain necessary amenities to the workers in terms of position of the worker in a particular society. It enables the male earner to provide for himself and his family, the necessities like food, clothing, shelter, including education for the children, protection against ill-health and other essential social needs.

BASIC WAGE PLANS

The basic wage plans for payments are :

Time Wage Plan

It pays employees based on the period of time for which they have been employed. When the quality of work is more important than the quantity and the nature of work cannot be easily standardized then a time wage system is preferred. Example, an organisation that follows the time wage system. Among the workers, if one produces 100 units in 10 hours and another, 80 units in 10 hours, both of them still get paid the same amount of wages. They are paid for the 10 hours of work, the number of units they produced is not relevant to their pay.

Under this system, the worker cannot earn more than a fixed amount. Since the worker's shifts and work schedules are pre-determined. The only way to earn more in this system is to work over-time or an extra shift if there is an organisational need.

Piece Wage Plan

Workers are paid for the work done. This method is employed when there is a need for production of large numbers.

In the case of time-wage plan, a certain level of productivity is expected whereas in piece –wage plan, some time limit is fixed.

Payment of Result

Under this system, the wage for each piece of work is fixed and the workers are paid once the work is completed

Skill-based Pay

This pay system is also called knowledge-based pay. According to American Compensation Association, skill-based pay is one of the fastest growing concepts in the U.S. and the same is true for Indian companies today. The employees are compensated for their job-related skills. Once, they gain extensive knowledge and new skills, they are promoted and rewarded with an increased pay.

Competency-based Pay

Competency can be defined as the knowledge, skills and behavior of an individual that contribute to a worker's performance. The employee is compensated for the competencies showing with the job. To implement the competency-based pay system in a bank, the best officer is selected and the characteristics that contribute to his performance are identified.

Broad Banding

It is a base-pay technique which reduces the number of salary levels into broad salary bands. If the salary band for the entry level is fixed as – Rs. 10,000-Rs. 18,000. The salary band for the next level can be Rs. 12,500-Rs. 2,000.

The advantage of broad banding is that it helps managers to fix the pay of individual workers, but within set limits. Also, it helps to avoid unnecessary distinctions in the organisation.

Variable Compensation

Also motivates individual workers to work effectively in groups. It is paid at different levels, the worker level, the manager level and the group level.

It makes employee responsible for their own pay packages, through their performance and contribution & this motivates improve their performance.

These programmes are designed to pay employees in accordance with their performance and not in accordance with their position in the organisational.

At the worker level, the worker is rewarded for achieving the production targets which motivates workers to improve their efficiency. At the manager level, the manager is rewarded for the achievement of results.

Executive Compensation

It is designed to attract and retain the chief executives of the company. It requires for planning in many sectors like-organisational structure, salary administration, short-term and long-term incentive plans, sales compensation, executive perquisites, retirement benefits. An HR professional design an executive compensation that attracts, retains and motivates executives in view of the above mentioned facts as well as market condition.

The following process can be adapted by an HR department to design an effective executive compensation plan.

1. to design a pay system that is linked to organisational objectives try to identify the flaws in the plan that have rendered it ineffective or inefficient.
2. to retain a competent and successful executive for a longer period of time the plan should provide an opportunity.
3. These plans must be made known to the stakeholders.

CONCEPT OF REWARDS

The reward system are linked to employee performance and commitment towards the organisation. These are extrinsic and intrinisic. Extrinsic rewards are feasible in nature and are under the control of the organisation. Examples, a promotion or a bonus. Intrinsic rewards are not feasible in nature and are internal to the individual also a challenging assignment or informal recognition. Rewards have also been classified as financial and non-financial.

Financial rewards are the rewards that employee receive in monetary terms. Example - a bonus or an annual incentive.

Non-financial rewards are intangible and are paid in kind. Example, the employee reaps the benefit of a subsidized cafeteria, though he is not paid in cash. Incentives are the rewards to an employee, his base wage or salary, in recognition of his performance and contribution. They can be termed as performance-based rewards. Example-annual performance incentives (monetary) and ESOP (Employee stock option plan).

INCENTIVE PLANS

There are two types of incentive plans: Short-term incentive plans, long-term incentive plans. Short-term plans are related to employee productivity over a short period of time, example, a day, a week. Long-term incentive plans are related to employee performance over a long period say, a year.

Short-term Plans

Generally, incentive plans are based on time rates or piece rates. Some of the incentive plans, based on these two methods:

(a) *Halsey Plan :* In this plan, an amount of work is fixed as a standard which is to be completed in a prescribed time. If the worker completes the work before the prescribed time then he gets a percentage of wages as extra earning. Example, a worker that completes the standard output in four hours, as the prescribed time in 6 hours. Let the hourly rate be Rs. 5 and the plan percentage of wages be fixed at 50%. Now, the extra wage that the worker receives may be calculated as : plan percentage, time saved, hourly rate.

(b) *Rowan Plan :* The worker is guaranteed a minimum wage on a time basis. Then a standard time is fixed for the completion of work and if the worker completes it before time, he earns more for the time saved. The extra earnings for the worker in the Rowan plan. Time saved*Time Taken*Hourly Rate/ Standard Time = (2*6*5) / 8 = 7.50.

(c) *Barth System of wages :* The workers are not guaranteed of a minimum rate.Wages are calculated as wages = standard time * time taken * hourly rate.Therefore, using the above formula, wages = 8*6*5 = 6.9*5 34.50.

(d) *Task Bonus System :* The task of each group member is pre-determined, one has to achieve it to earn a bonus above his standard pay. A bonus is paid over and above the time wage if the standard task is accomplished.

(e) *Point-rating system :* Each job is rated in terms of a standard time. Let an organisation fix its standard time value 10 units of production per hour. The number of working hours per day be 8 and the hourly rate be Rs. 6. At the end of the day, if a worker produces 100 units. This is equivalent to 10 hours of production as per the standard time value. Therefore, the worker is paid Rs. 60 @ Rs 5/hr.

Long-Term Plans

Long term plans help in providing steady earnings. Examples of long-term incentive plans are annual bonus, profit sharing gain sharing, ESOPs, etc.

(a) *Annual bonus :* The annual bonus is based on the annual performance of the company. The factors that determine the bonus are the company profits and the performance of the group. In many organisation in government agencies bonus is paid at the time of a major festival. For example, employees of many firms and government service get their 'Holi bonus' every year before the festival.

An employer is bound to pay to every employee a minimum bonus which shall be 8.33 per cent of the salary earned by the employee during the accounting year one hundred rupees, whichever is higher, whether or not the employee has any allocable surplus in the accounting year.

(b) *Profit-sharing :* The employees earn a share of the company's profit, which is normally calculated as a percentage of the total profit. There are three major types of profit-sharing plans.

(c) *Distribution plan :* In this plan annual quarterly cash bonus is paid according to a pre-determined formula based on the company profits.

(d) *Deferred plan :* A plan where employees earn profit-sharing credits instead of cash payment, which are distributed when the employee parts with the organisation.

(e) *Combination plan :* The plan is a combination of the distribution and deferred plans.

(f) *Gain-sharing :* In this method of incentive payment, the group is rewarded for its team-work, coordination and other characteristics that have determined its success.

(g) *Employee Stock Plans :* In this scheme employees are given a part of ownership at a price lower than market price, in consideration of their duration and/ or meritorious performance on the job.

The different types of employees stock plans are explained below:

- *Employee Stock Purchase Plan (ESPP) :* In this scheme the employees are given the right to acquire shares of the company immediately after they earn them normally at a price lower than the prevailing market price.
- *Restricted Stock Plan :* In this type of stock plan, the employees need not to put in money. One of the major restrictions is that the share may be fake if they are not "earned out" over a specific period of time.
- *Employee Stock Option Scheme (ESOS)* : In this plan the company grants an option to its employees to acquire shares at a future date. And the options are offered at a pre-determined rate.
- *Stock Appreciation Rights (SAR)/Phantom Shares:* Here, the employee does not have to put in any money and has the right to reqlinquish the stock.
- *Phantom Stock :* It is a special type of ESOP that protects the holder against any depreciation in the value of the stock.

- *Premium priced options :* These are also known as performance vesting options. These are applicable if the market price of the stock reaches or exceeds the pre-determined exercise price, which is significantly higher than the current market price.

NON MONETARY INCENTIVES

It is one of the best methods of motivating employee by giving non-monetary incentive for their performance and contribution. Some of the non-monetary incentives are:

(*i*) Recognition of an employee's contribution.

(*ii*) Rewarding an employee for his performance through free gifts of free vacations boosts his morale.

(*iii*) A challenging assignment given to an employee increases the management's confidence in his abilities.

(*iv*) Giving additional responsibility to an employee acts in much the same way as a challenging assignment.

CHARACTERISTICS FOR INCENTIVE PLANS

The characteristics for an incentive plan are as follows:

(*i*) The incentive plan should be linked to employee performance should be communicated to the employees.

(*ii*) The inputs and employee suggestions should be valued and rewarded.

(*iii*) The incentive plan should be minimally affected by external factors like the stock market performance industry's performance.

(*iv*) The incentive plan of an organisation should provide a challenge to the employees and should be flexible.

(*v*) The organisational incentive plan should also benefit the management with tangible savings in labor costs.

(*vi*) The incentive plan should include both monetary and non-monetary incentives for employees.

Employee Benefits

Benefits are normally not linked to performance of the employee. It is like the fringe benefits that accumulates to an employee over his salary.. There are some common employee benefits like :

- *Medical facilities to the employee and his family:* Employees and their family members are provided medical facilities, free of cost.
- *Paid holiday/vacation to the employee and his family :* Employees get a paid holiday, normally every year. In some the company even pays for the vacation of the employee with his family.
- *Retiral benefits like PF and gratuity :* It is mandatory for the organisation to pay retiral benefits, PF and gratuity to the employee.
- *Employee insurance :* Employees have to be insured for life and against accident or illness, under the Employee State Insurance Act.
- *Educational allowance for employee's children:* The organisation provides a fixed educational allowance towards the school-related expenses of the employees' children.
- *Merit Scholarships for employees' children :* Organisations encourage the children of employees to excel in their studies awarding merit scholarships.
- *Company accommodation :* Many organisations provide subsidized quarters for their employees.
- *Company transportation facilities :* Many organiza-tions provide transportation facilities to their workforce. Like buses, company cars.
- *Cafeteria and rest rooms :* Companies provide cafete-rias to their employees with free or subsidized coffee/ tea/snacks.

- *Study leave :* Many organisations provide study leave to their employees to gain more knowledge and earn higher qualifications.
- *Recreational facilities :* The recreational facilities provided by organisation vary from a TV room to a well-equipped gym and can include facilities for yoga, sports, games and weekend parties.
- *Credit cards :* Organisations tie up with credit card companies and help employees get credit cards at a subsidized fee.
- *Business and Professional memberships :* Organisations pay to the professional membership fee of their employee.
- *Tax assistance :* Organisations spare their employees from tax planning hassles providing professional assistance to them.
- *Interest free loans :* many organisations provide their employees interest free loans.

MODEL QUESTIONS

1. Explain Job evaluation and its objectives.
2. What are the steps involved in Job evaluation?
3. Explain Different types of wages.
4. Please explain all the types of wage plan necessary for wage payment.
5. Explain executive compensation and its objective.

CHAPTER

10 Grievance Handling

CONCEPT

A grievance is a sign of an employee's dissatisfaction, either with the job or the organisation. It is a complaint affecting one or more workers. There are many reasons to arise a grievance such as – if there is a gap between employee expectations and organisational rewards then it normally leads to a grievance. If there is an unpleasant relationship with the supervisor then sometimes it leads to a grievance.

When an employee has a grievance and takes it to the management, the grievance redressal authority must analyze it to identify the root cause. If the management fails to take necessary corrective action, the employee's morale and his performance gets affected.

According to Dale S. Breach: "Grievance is any dissatisfaction or feeling of injustice in connection with one's employment situation that is brought to the attention of management."

Causes

It may be classified like the following :

1. Grievance resulting out of working conditions:
    - tight production standard,
    - poor relationship with the supervisor,
    - no availability of proper tools and machines.

2. Grievance resulting from management policy:
    - wage rates,
    - overtime,
    - seniority,
    - transfer,
    - promotion,
    - lack of career planning, and
    - leave.
3. Grievance resulting from personal maladjustment :
    - excessive self-esteem,
    - over-ambition, and
    - impractical attitude to life.
4. Grievance arising from illegal violation of :
    - Central or State laws,
    - the collective bargaining agreement, and
    - company rules and regulations.

Grievance Settlement

The following conditions are necessary for a grievance settlement procedure :

1. Resolves the issue without any delay.
2. No violation of organisational rules and policies.
3. Identifies the root cause for employee grievence.
4. Resolves the issue at the lowest possible level.
5. Resolves the issue in an amicable manner.
6. Provides data and information of employee grievances.
7. Follow up the redressal procedure to provide the current status to the employee and the management.
8. Helps the management to identify the core issues.
9. Provides unbiased and objective redressal of employee grievances.

10. Is a short and simple procedure that can be easily understood.
11. Considers the legal, social, financial and psychological aspects for a settlement.

Benefits of a Grievance Settlement

These are the following benefits to an organisation because of its grievance settlement procedure :

- It helps the management to win the trust and confidence of the employees.
- If the grievance does not satisfy the employee, he approaches to the next level.
- In the absence of a grievance redressal system, an employee either keep his dissatisfaction to himself or share it with his colleagues.
- A good grievance helps to maintain harmonious industrial relations as employee grievances are settled before they turn into industrial conflicts and have a check on arbitrary actions.
- Grievance procedures helps to have a check on arbitrary actions. As a result, supervisors usually do not indulge in baised decisions.
- Employees are free to express their discontentment, problems or frustrations to the top management.
- Previous experiences gained in grievance redressal system helps the management to take into consideration the problems that may be encountered by the employees and to formulate plans like plant expansion or installation of latest technology.

Grievance Settlement Procedure

According to the National Commission on Labor the procedure for grievance settlement as:

1. In the first stage, the employee conveys his grievance verbally to his supervisor. If the supervisor fails to respond within the prescribed time limit of 48 hours,

the employee approaches the next level in the settlement procedure.

2. At this stage, the employee fills up the grievance settlement form of the company and approaches the head of his department with this form. The head of the department within three days make a settlement, in case of failure the grievance reaches the next stage.
3. The third stage of the settlement procedure is the Grievance Committee. The committee is given seven days to discuss the issue with the employee and reach a settlement. In case of a unanimous decision, the management has to implement it. The management is given three days time to communicate its decision, otherwise the grievance is taken to the fourth stage.
4. In the fourth stage, the representatives of employee and the department appeal to the management to review its decision. The management has a week's time to revise its decision. In case, there is no change in the decision, the issue may be referred to the union.
5. In the last stage, the union discuss the issue and tries to make a settlement between the grievant employee and the management. In case of the union's failure to do so, the grievance reaches the last stage of the grievance procedure.

Grievance Redressal Procedure in Unionised Organisations

Steps of the grievance settlement procedure in a unionised organisation.

- At this stage the grievance may be settled if the supervisor has the requisite people management skills and problem solving skills. If the employee is not satisfied with the settlement then he approaches to his manager and conveys his problem. Who may forward this grievance to a higher level of manager or departmental head after hearing.

- If the decision at this level is also not acceptable to the employee, then the grievance is referred to the grievance committee. The committee can ask the employee to accept the proposed settlement of the employer.
- The final step is when the grievance is referred to the arbitrator. The decision of the arbitrator should be acceptable to both the management and the employee.

The grievance settlement procedure in non-unionised organisations, is different from the procedure explained above in unionized organisations.

If an employee moves to office of his superior to express dissatisfaction or a grievance that he has. The management makes effort to make him satisfied and motivated.

Legal Aspects of the Grievance Redressal Procedure in India

The Indian Labor Conference in 1957 decided to formulate a satisfactory grievance settlement procedure like :

Conformity with existing legislation : A grievance procedure must be acceptable to both the employer and employees and it should be designed to supplement the existing statutory provisions.

Sophisticated machinery : A grievance should be addressed as soon as possible, because a delay in the process further demotivate the employees.

Awareness of employee to grievance procedure : The employees should have a good knowledge and should know whom they have to approach with their grievance, the different stages involved and the time limit etc. If the grievance is not solved at this level, then it can be taken to the grievance committee comprising of the representatives of management and workers.

Recognised union : If, there is a recognised union in an organisation then in such a case grievance committee consists of two representatives from the management and two representatives from the union. One union representatives should be from the department in which the concerned employee works.

If there is no recognised union, but only a Work Committee, then the grievance committee may have two representatives from the management, one representative from the department in which the employee works on the Work Committee and the other representative a secretary or the vice president of the works committee.

Conflict Resolution

In a conflict, if no challenging questions are posed to the management, some of it's decisions, which are counter productive may affect the organisation and its performance. Thus, managers should accept the occurrence of conflict and recognize those grievances that may aid organisational renewal.

Although, conflict is faced in different ways but there are some basic aspects that people respond to it are :

Withdrawal : Those who can't face confrontations withdraw from the situation rather than face it and are usually sensitive to their own feeling and also to others' feelings.

Willingful : Those people who suppress their own needs, opinions, feelings, interests in order to resolve the conflict in an amicable manner.

Arbitration : In the case of arbitration, the decision of the arbitrator is final.

Mediation : The mediation party do not pass any judgement but looks forward on the two disputing parties towards a mutually acceptable settlement.

Compromising : In order to reach an agreement each of the parties make a few compromises to reach a commonly acceptable settlement.

Cordial relationships : To maintain cordial relationships define the needs of both the parties and then try to meet those needs

MODEL QUESTIONS

1. What is grievance?
2. Explain the benefits of grievance settlement.
3. What are the steps involved in grievance settlement?
4. Explain procedure for grievance settlement in unionised organisation.
5. Discuss conflict resolution and the methods to deal it.

CHAPTER

11

Disciplinary Action

CONCEPT

The employees who do not follow the organisational rules and regulations such as come late for work, indulge in fights with co-workers, sometimes come drunk to work, break the safety rules etc. The human resource manager has to consider these sensitive types of problems. Such behaviour of the employees not only affects their own performance rather it affects the performance of other employees as well. So, it is necessary that indiscipline should be handled immediately as it affects the performance and morale of the entire work group. Because, the employees should stick to the rules and regulations made by the organisations to ensure order and discipline. Moreover, when employees involve in indiscipline, the organisation is forced to punish them to discourage such behavior.

According to a scientist, Nirmal Singh, "Discipline is employees self-control which prompts him to willingly co-operate with the organisational objectives, rules, standard etc."

Objectives of Discipline

The objectives of discipline are:

- To provide direction to the employees and to improve organisational performance
- To ensure and enable employees to work in accordance with the rules and regulations of the organisations.

- To maintain a sense of orderliness and conformity, trust and confidence.

The success of any disciplinary procedure depends on the cooperation of both the employer and the employee and their mutual trust.

So, it is the responsibility of the supervisors to make the employees aware of the need to maintain organisational discipline and the implication of indiscipline.

Types of Dicipline

Discipline among employees can be classified into two types either through rewards or through penalties as:

Positive Discipline

It is also known as cooperative discipline or determinative discipline. If employees are motivated through rewards and appreciation according to organisational rules and regulations, is termed as positive discipline. It gives emphasis on the concept of self-discipline and self-control. When employees develop mutual respect for each other and the organisational rules and procedures. It happens when they understand and believe that these rules and procedures contribute to the achievement of organisational goals as well as their personal goals.

Negative Discipline

It makes the employee strictly follow the rules and discipline due to some fear like, fear for loss of promotion, an increment or a job. So, unwillingly they try to admit to the organizational rules. It involves the use of techniques like reprimands, lay-offs, demotions or transfers.

Misconduct

Misconduct destroys its reputation and develops unrest in the employees. If not tackled immediately, these acts can lead to disciplinary problems like:

Minor infractions : Though, it cause little harm but if neglected can result in serious problems for the organisation. They may be related to coming late to work, negligence to work etc.

Major infractions : Mainly it affects the morale of the employees as well as orderly operation of the organisation. These may be related to cheating, stealing, violating safety regulations etc.

Intolerable infractions : It creates serious harm and damage to the organisation. Such as use of alcohol while at work, smoking in the workplace etc.

The basic acts of misconduct are :

Attendance : The attendance must be maintained but it has become one of the basic and major problems that managers faces in organisations. This is more prevalent among unskilled/semi-skilled workers and junior management level employees. The reasons for attendance problems can be:

- Incongruence in employee and organisational goals,
- Personality characteristics, like attitude towards work,
- Unpleasant relationship with supervisors and co-workers, and
- Ensured job security.

On-the Job Behaviour : The behaviour of the employees must be conducive to the rules and regulations designed by the organisation. Any behaviour that affects the work of the individual or other employees demands disciplinary action. The following reasons may be conducive :

- Lack of proper upbringing and education
- Work-related pressures and strained relationships
- General attitude and personality of the individual.

Dishonesty : It means distrust among employees and between management and employees. It makes an employee to remain aloof with the organisation or *vice versa*. The resons for dishonesty may be considered as :

- Social and economic pressures;
- Lack of proper upbringing and education;
- Personality characteristics of the employees;

Activities: The activities are those features of the employees wherein he remains engaged and which affect either their on-the job performance or the organisation's reputation. Activities such as unauthorised strikes, criminal activities and working for a competitor etc reflect it.

Causes of Misconduct

It is disorderliness at work and non-conformity to the prescribed rules and regulations of the management. Some of the causes of indiscipline or misconduct are:

- Improper or inconvenient working conditions and social and economic conditions can lead to acts of indiscipline by workers.
- Strained relationships with the supervisor or with colleagues can force an employee to indulge in acts of indiscipline.
- Improper or biased evolution of individuals and their performance can result in demotivated employees.
- Loss of trust or confidence in each other or in the management can make employees behave in an indiscipline manner.
- Lack of proper education and upbringing of the workers can also lead to indiscipline at work.

Principles of Maintaining Discipline

The disciplinary procedure must be fair and acceptable to all the employees because it has serious implication for its employees. So the following steps must be taken care off like:

- The rules and regulations should be framed with mutual coordination and acceptance of the management and employees and must be evaluated and updated time to time.
- Rules should be formulated based on the nature of work and working conditions.
- The rules should be so formulated that they ensure an objective and unbiased analysis of the acts of indiscipline.
- All the employees should know the penalties for violation of different rules.
- The disciplinary procedure should provide an analysis of a rule or its violation.

Disciplinary Procedure

To incorporate all the principles, disciplinary procedure should be implemented in different stages and not in a single stage. The stages are discussed below:

(i) *Charge sheet :* when the management of an organisation initiates an enquiry against an employee for the misconduct, the concerned employee is issued a charge sheet. The charge sheet indicates the charge against the employee and seek an explanation for the employee's misconduct. The management can issue a show cause notice before issuing a charge sheet to get an explanation from the employee.

(ii) *Explanation*: If the employee admits his misconduct or if the management is satisfied with the explanation given by the employee in response to the charge-sheet, then in such a case no future enquiry is made.

(iii) *Notice of Enquiry :* A notice of enquiry must be issued to the worker after taking the decision. The notice must mention the time, date and place of enquiry. An enquiry officer is also appointed, preferably a person well-versed in law or an outside expert conversant with the intricacies and procedures of domestic enquiries.

(iv) *Holding a full-fledged enquiry* : The employee concerned must be given an opportunity to be heard if the enquiry is conducive. In some cases. If it is felt that the offence is serious or the employee concerned may influence the enquiry proceedings, he may either be asked to go on leave or may be suspended with or without pay, pending the enquiry.

(v) *Final order of Action :* Based on the findings of the enquiry officer the appropriate authority either acquits the employee or declare him guilty of the charges. Based on the decision taken, the manager should consider the employees previous record, precedent and the effects of this action on other employees.

(vi) *Follow-up :* The follow-up must be taken up properly to make the order of punishment effective.

APPROACHES TO DISCIPLINE

There are three main approaches to discipline. They are incorrect discipline, Preventive and positive discipline.

Incorrect Discipline

The term 'incorrect discipline' refers to the usage of inappropriate measures to enforce discipline in the organisation. Some of the inappropriate techniques used by manager are:

Punitive Discipline : It is also referred to as negative discipline which assumes the employees to work more effectively and with discipline if fear is instilled in them. This kind of disciplinary approach is less in use now, because of the protection of the employees by unions and government legislation.

Negative Feedback : In the organisations where employees are given feedback only when their performance is found to be unsatisfactory. If an employee performs well his performance is not recognised or acknowledged, and no feedback is given. This kind of approach, called the negative feedback approach, that demotivates employees. Hence, it is important for organisations to give both positive and negative feedback to employees to enable them evaluate their own performance.

Late Intervention : If the manager ignores indiscipline and allows the problem to continue, is referred to late intervention. In the initial stages it must be identified by an employee and the necessary corrective action should be taken to solve it.

Labeling Employees not Behaviour : Often, managers label employees because of their unsatisfactory performance on a job which has negative implications. As, the employee may carry the label over to other jobs and work units and the label may serve as a self-fulfilling prophecy. Second, such labeling focuses only on the employee and not on his act of indiscipline.

Misplaced Responsibility : Sometimes, it is analysed that the management is responsible for the misconduct of the employee not the employee.

Preventive Discipline

In this aspect managers take extra care to see that employees are satisfied and do not indulge in any activity that leads to indiscipline in the workplace. This kind of disciplinary approach is proactive in nature. It has some characteristics as:

- The manager should make sure while selecting that the employee goals are in congruence with the organisational goals.

- The training and development of employees adapt themselves to the job requirement to deliver good performance.
- The management should explain the disciplinary procedure and constructive feedback to the employee.

Positive Discipline

It makes the employees to realize their behavior through constructive feedback. Then they are helped to overcome their shortcomings with adequate support from the mangers. This type of disciplinary process is positive and facilitates problem solving in a people oriented approach. It has a series of policies and steps as-

Responsibility for ensuring discipline: Some organisations give the authority to the immediate supervisors, while others feel that doing so it may result in inconsistency in application of discipline. So, a solution for this may be that HR staff take the responsibility of ensuring discipline. There is one disadvantage that HR staff have to spend a considerable amount of time on disciplinary matters. Another disadvantage is that they may lose control over their subordinates.

The best possible solution is to give the superior the authority to administer less severe disciplinary actions like written and verbal warning. And punishments like suspension or dismissal, the supervisor and the HR representative may take action in consultation with each other.

Communicating the organisational policies, procedures and rules: To maintain satisfactory levels of employee performance the management must clearly communicate all its policies, procedures and rules to the employees. This information can be communicated by the following methods:

- Employee hand books;
- Orientation programs;

- Union contracts;
- Rules and regulations distributed in writing;
- Rules and regulations posted on bulletin boards;
- Superior-subordinate discussion of job standards, company policies and procedures.

Communicate the Expected Performance: The managers must communicate all the disciplinary procedure to the employees while formulating that is expected from the employees. It should be communicated to the employees in a simple and lucid style. Punishing an employee for indiscipline is unwise, unless the management has clearly defined the standards of discipline and good performance.

Collecting Valid Information : A through analysis must be made regarding the allegations made before taking any action against an employee for misconduct. If valid information is collected about employee's wrongdoing then it makes disciplinary procedure effective and easier to administer.It is important to collect facts because an employee may improve his or her behavior if evidence of violation of rules are shown.

Monitoring Progressive Discipline : Even the appropriate disciplinary action may vary depending on the situation but it is generally desirable for discipline to be progressive. The important characteristics of progressive discipline are :

- an appropriate penalty for the offence, and
- a series of increasingly serious penalties

Monitoring corrective counseling: The objective of positive disciplinary action is not to rule out punishment but to correct an employee's undesirable behaviour at the right time.

To be effective, it is necessary that the employees' supervisor offer support, encouragement and assistance to the employee. The corrective counseling differs from traditional techniques because the superior avoids telling the employee how to solve his problems. Instead, he helps him to determine the most effective way to solve the problem.

TYPES OF DISCIPLINARY ACTION

The various disciplinary actions that are administered in response to prominent acts of indiscipline by employees are verbal warning, written warning, suspension, pay cut, demotion and dismissal.

Verbal Warning

In verbal warning the supervisor explain to the employee, the rule that has been violated and the implication for violating it. The supervisor or manager make efforts to find out the reason for the employee making violation of the rule and ask for possible alternative solutions to the problem. If the solutions offered by the employee are not suitable, then the manager can help him to find ways to avoid the problem in the future.

Written Warning

Written warning is placed in the employee's file and a copy given to the employee and one sent to the personnel department. The employee is informed of the violation, its effect and consequences of future violations. The only difference between the two actions is that the manager tells the employees that a written warning will be issued. He writes down the rule that has been violated, any assurances given by the employee that he will correct his behavior, and the further action will be administered if the deviant behavior is repeated.

Suspension

Suspension is the last stage if the employee does not stick to the rules and regulations of the organisation in spite of being given a verbal and written warning.

In suspension, the employee is released from work for a short period of time and he is not paid during this time. This kind of action helps the employee to realise his fault and the inconvenience that his behavior has caused to others in the workplace.

Demotion

After suspension, if the management feels no improvement in the performance of the employee then in such a case demotion may be an alternative. There are very few organisations that use this step as a disciplinary action. Because, it may demoralize not only to the employee but his co-workers as well. It is administered only when

- The employee ability is not suitable to the job.
- Management perceives itself legally or ethically constrained from dismissing the employee.
- It is sure that the action will aware employees to change his behavior.

Pay Cut

This aspect has a demoralizing effect on the employees, but is considered a rational action by the management if the other alternative is only dismissal.

Dismissal

The dismissal or discharge means the termination of employment initiated by the employer. The reasons to the dismissal of an employee are :

- excessive absenteeism.
- Serious misconduct
- False statement of the qualification at the time of employment
- Theft of company's property.

Before, discharging an employee of his duties the following conditions must be satisfied:

- After being filed a charge-sheet against the employee, an enquiry should be conducted regarding the misconduct and it should be fair and prior notice of the time.

- The order must be communicated to the employee against whom it has been passed.
- The enquiry officer should record the findings based on recorded evidence.
- The finding must be based on recorded evidence and should not be biased.
- The order of dismissal or discharge of the employee must be passed in good faith.

Enforcement of Dicipline Norms

It is a set of self-imposed mutually agreed voluntary principles of discipline and good relations between the management and the workers in industry.

The discipline norms in the Indian industry was formulated on the recommendations of the Indian Labour Conference held in New Delhi in the year 1957. The code was made applicable to the industry from 1st June 1958. Its main aim was to explain certain principles of discipline that govern the Indian industry. The basic features of this are as follows:

- Both the management and the employees should follow certain self-imposed rules in order to avoid disputes.
- Each party should acknowledge and respect each other's rights and responsibilities.
- No party should take any unilateral decision regarding any disputes.
- The code discourages litigation and lays emphasis on settlement of disputes through negotiation, conciliation and voluntary arbitration.
- There should be precise and speedy implementation of disciplinary action and any reached agreement.
- Employees and trade unions can take appropriate actions in case they find officers and supervisors indulging in activities which are against the code.

- The trade union must be recognised in accordance with the criteria explained for this purpose.

Industrial Employment (Standing Orders) Act, 1946

The primary objective of the Industrial Employment (Standing Orders) Act, 1946 is to ensure protection of labour providing uniform and stable working conditions of service. Prior to this act, the terms and conditions of employment were vague and unknown to employees. These terms and conditions were changed and misused frequently. This act was enacted to address these problems.

The Industrial Employment (Standing Orders) Act, 1946 expects from the employers to define clearly, the conditions of employment, or service rules, and to make them known to the workmen employed by them.

The Central and State Governments have prescribed the Model Standing Orders to serve as the basic foundation of the rules of conduct. Industrial establishment either draft their own standing orders on the basis of the model standing orders, and get them certified by the concerned authorities or simply adopt the model standing orders.

The employer of industrial establishment prepares the draft of the standing orders converging all the matter specified in the Model Standing Orders. He gives five copies of the draft to the certifying officer, along with an application in the prescribed format. In the prescribed format particulars like details of the employees in the establishments, and the trade union, if any, to which they belong to is be submitted. The application is submitted within six months from the date the Act becomes applicable in the establishment.

If a question arises about the application or interpretation of any certified standing order, it may be referred by the employer, employee or the trade union to a labour court established for the administration of such procedures. The labour court, after listening to the concerned parties makes a decision which is final and binding on all the parties involved.

Factories Act, 1948

In 1948, the Act was replaced to regulate working conditions. It lays down basic minimum requirements for the safety, health and welfare of factory workers. It is applicable to industries and factories employing 10 or more persons in India. The Factories Act, 1948 provides for the appointment of a Welfare Officer in every factory employing 500 or more workers. These welfare officers also look after complaints and grievance of workers. However, these provisions are not helpful due to the dual role which these officers are called upon to play. In 1911, the hours of work were regulated and incorporated in the act. In 1934, on the recommendations of Royal Commission of Labour this act was amended. This act insists that the following preventive measures must be adopted like : Cleanliness, ventilation, no overcrowding, proper drinking water supply, provision for first aid boxes.

The Industrial Disputes Act, 1947

The Industrial Disputes Act, provides :

- The employer in relation to every industrial establishment in which fifty or more workmen are employed shall provide for a grievance settlement authority.
- When an industrial dispute connected with an individual workman arises in an establishment, of which such workman is a member may refer such disputes to the grievance settlement authority for settlement.
- The grievance settlement authority shall follow such procedure and complete it's proceedings within such period as may be prescribed.
- No reference shall be made to Boards, Courts or tribunals of any dispute referred to in this section unless such dispute has been referred to the Grievance Settlement Authority concerned and the decision of the authority is not acceptable to any of the parties to the dispute.

Under section 2-A of the Industrial Disputes Act, the term 'industrial disputes' includes all differences between an industrial workman and his employer connected with, organizing out of his discharge, dismissal, retrenchment or termination not withstanding that no other workman nor any union or workman is a party to dispute.

MODEL QUESTIONS

1. Explain the aims and objectives of the discipline.
2. Discuss various types of discipline.
3. Focuss on disciplinary procedure and its approaches.
4. What are the types of disciplinary action?
5. Write notes on Incorrect discipline, preventive discipline and positive discipline.
6. Write notes on Industrial employment Act,1948 and Industrial Disputes Act,1947.

CHAPTER 12

Employee Relations and Collective Bargaining

CONCEPT

The past decade of twentieth century, faced the start of new era in the history of industrial relations in the country. The number of working days lost due to strikes and lock-outs reduced. This can be attributed to change in the attitudes of management and employees.

Industrial relations can be defined as the relationship between the management and the employees of an industry.

According to encyclopaedia, the concept of industrial relations denotes the relations of the state with employees, workers and their organisations.

From different definitions it can be concluded that industrial relations:

- the outcome of employer-employee relationship.
- facilitate harmonious relationships in an organization.
- based on mutual compromise and adjustment, for the benefit of both the parties involved.

ROLES IN INDUSTRIAL RELATIONS

In an enterprise, where employees do the work and the management takes decisions on behalf of the employers, the interests of the employees are represented by the trade unions/associations. Unions/associations play multifarious role in protecting the interests of the employees.

Employees

The employees must be satisfied with the organisation, it's policies, procedures and their jobs if harmonious industrial relations have to be maintained, because, employees are the base of organisations. Their dissatisfaction may lead to industrial conflicts. So, it is important that employee-friendly policies and rules must be framed to provide a conductive work environment and quality of work life to the employees.

Trade Unions

It negotiates with the management in the interests of the employees, at the organisational level or at the industry level. It enjoys the power and status based on the support of the employees.

In India there are number of central labour organisations such Indian National Trade Union Congress (INTUC), All India Trade Union Congress (AITUC), National Labour Organization (NLO), and the Centre of Indian Trade Union (CITU), to which a large number of organizational level trade unions/associations are affiliated. These organisations represent and protect the interests of their members on all important issues that affect the workers' interests.

As State agents they act in socialist countries and work in coordination with the management to improve employee productivity. Also, take welfare work, social insurance schemes, provision of sickness and disablement benefits, arranging holiday camps. There are different committees such as works committees, Joint Management Councils and Worker Representatives on the Board of Directors in India, where worker participation in management occurs.

Management Policies

The management policies help to maintain high employee morale and to prevent industrial conflicts and disputes. The role of the management in industrial relations has undergone a transformation from an exploitative authoritative style to a more participative style at the different stages.

Authoritative Position

The management was leading an authoritative position and was paying to workers disproportionately. The working conditions were pathetic with the absence of basic amenities like water. The management enforced a strict discipline and any breach was punished severely.

Benevolent Style

In this style, the management was kind, but strict towards the workers. This change in style was mainly due to the demands from the trade unions and the protection of government laws.

Consultative Management Style

This style followed information-sharing, consultation with the unions and collective bargaining etc. Management was forced to introduce a two way communication channel with the employees. With the result it facilitated a free flow of communication downwards, upwards and laterally.

Participating Style

In the participating style of management, employees are considered in all aspects of management, from determining the strategy to identifying the objectives and from planning the execution to implementing the decisions.

The Government

The government provides a basic framework within which the management, trade unions and the employees are expected to work for the common good of the organization.

OBJECTIVES

The objectives of industrial relations are:

(*i*) To ensure discipline in the organization.

(*ii*) To protect the interests of the labour and the management.

(*iii*) To develop standard of living and mutual understanding.

(*iv*) To maintain industrial peace and harmony.

(*v*) To increase productivity and the bargaining capacity of the workers.

(*vi*) To provide a basic framework for the management and the employees to resolve their differences.

INDUSTRIAL DISPUTES PREVENTION MACHINERY

To maintain harmonious industrial relations management and workers enhance productivity; and help the organization focus on preventing industrial disputes.

There are various ways and means to prevent industrial disputes as:

1. **Worker Participation :** It enhance their commitment and loyalty for the organization. It is encouraged because it allows the employees to get involved in the management decisions. An employer employing hundred or more worker is required to create a Works Committee comprising of representatives from the management and the workers.
2. **Employee Grievance Redressal Machinery :** It helps the management to prevent individual grievances from taking the shape of industrial disputes.
3. **Voluntary Arbitration :** The arbitrator is chosen by mutual agreement of both the parties whose decision is final which has to be abided by both the parties.
4. **Counciliation :** Counciliation is the next stage if the management and the unions fail to resolve their differences through collective bargaining or arbitration. The conciliator facilities the agreement of both the parties offering advice and consultancy.
5. **Court of Enquiry :** The court of enquiry is constituted by the government to inquire into the dispute and come

out with the facts of the dispute. The court does not have any power to give its verdict on the dispute rather it only assists the process of conciliation.

6. **Tripartile bodies :** It is similar to bodies as - Indian Labour Congress, standing labour committee and industrial committee help the government in setting the industrial disputes through agreements.

7. **Adjudication :** Adjudication is the last resort, if an industrial dispute leads to strike, lock-out or temporary suspension of activities of the organization. There is legal binding on both the parties if the decision is taken at this stage. The different stages of adjudication are:

   (*i*) **Labour Courts :** With the help of State government it is constituted for settlement of industrial disputes. It deals with matters related to standing order application and interpretation, discharge or dismissal of a worker and a strike or a lock out.

   (*ii*) **Industrial Tribunal :** It deals with all the matters within the jurisdiction of labour courts and matters related to compensation, work hours and shifts, leaves and holidays, payment of bonus, provident and gratuity, discipline, retrenchment and closure of the establishment.

   (*iii*) **National Tribunal :** It is constituted when an industrial dispute affects more than one state in the country or when the firm in question operates in more than one state.

CONCEPT OF COLLECTIVE BARGAINING

Collective bargaining is a managerial tool that facilitates an amicable and mutually acceptable agreement between the management and the employees, to solve all employment-related problems. In some cases, the intervention by the third party is necessary to resolve these matters.

It was developed by Sydney Web and Beatrice Web, who believed that collective bargaining was equivalent to individual bargaining, whose primary aim was to achieve economic advantage. This viewpoint of them was popularly known as the 'critical viewpoint'.

The conditions that favour collective bargaining are:

- There should be a single union or in case of multiple unions, those must be a common agreement among them.
- Management should follow the requests of the trade unions and should identify the representatives of the trade unions.
- The culture of the organization should have the right spirit for the collective bargaining to be successful.
- The role of a third party should be minimized and agreements should be based on bipartite bargaining.
- All the parties involved should aim at a win-win situation and not a win-lose situation.

FEATURES OF COLLECTIVE BARGAINING

The main features of collective bargaining are:

Group Activity

It is a group activity because the parties involved in the bargaining process represent different groups – the employees and the management. The employees are represented by their union delegates and the management through their team of designated officials.

Levels

There are different levels in the process of collective bargaining. Staring from a simple bipartite discussion to national level between management and the employee at unit or plant level.

Flexibility

The flexibility in ideas and opinions, demands and requests and decisions and agreements is the chief characteristic of the collective bargaining process.

Win-win Situation

All the parties involved should have a win-win attitude and aim to reach an agreement that is in the best interests of all the parties.

Strong Relationships

The collective bargaining, helps to build strong relationships between the management and the employees. Moreover, it results in designing and implementing contracts of employment between the management and the trade unions.

Characteristics of Art and Science

It shows both the characteristics of science and arts. Because, if someone is an expert at collective bargaining means he has practiced the art well. Also, a science because it helps someone in better negotiation and good performance.

OBJECTIVES OF COLLECTIVE BARGAINING

Collective bargaining has benefits not only for the present, but also for the future:

- To reach a solution that is acceptable.
- To resolve conflicts and disputes in a mutually agreeable manner, if possible through third party.
- To prevent any conflict in the future through mutually signed contracts.
- To develop a conducive atmosphere to have good industrial relations.
- To enhance the productivity of the organization.

According to Prof. Butler, it is the function of collective bargaining under three heads:

A Process of social change : It is a process of social change, that helps to restructure the power hierarchy of competing groups.

A Peace treaty : It serves as a peace treaty between both the parties in case of continued conflict.

A system of 'industrial jurisprudence' – It formulates terms and conditions and accordingly labor and management will cooperate and work together for a specific period.

STAGES IN COLLECTIVE BARGAINING

Phase of Pre-negotiation : This stages tarts before the onset of the collective bargaining phase, under this the management estimates the strength and ability of various labour unions. During this stage, all the data information and figures which are relevant, are collected for the preset of the negotiation.

Negotiator's selection : Here, both the management and labour unions select their representatives who kill take part in negotiations from both the side respectively. The representatives who are selected as negotiators are fully acquainted with the issues for which the negotiations are to be done.

Bargaining strategy : This is the phase where the management decides basic strategies and policies which are to be followed in future at the time of bargaining with the employees. Similarly, labour unions should also make clear their strategies and intentions on which their negotiations will be based. Moreover, everything should be made clear from both the sides is management and the union, before heading towards the bargaining table.

Bargaining technique : This technique is based upon the principle of 'Give and Take' involving both the management and the labour union. Here, both the party should try to acquire as much advantage as possible. The contracts are discussed from all the point and then the decisions are reviewed. If needed government mediators can also be involved.

Agreement : In this stage both the parties involved enters into a collective and mutual agreement. These agreements are made for a given period of time. These agreement give detail information of security of job, grievance handling procedure, promotion policy, transfer policy, rules regarding layoff, rules regarding retrenchment, hours of work, rules regarding leaves, incentive schemes security and health, managerial liability.

Implementation of agreement : This is the final stage of collective bargaining. Here, the agreement formed is implemented involving both the management and the labour union. Both the parties honor these agreements and implement them sinerely.

CONCEPT OF WORKERS' PARTICIPATION IN MANAGEMENT

Participation management refers to the process of involving employees or employees representatives at all levels of decision making process. Workers participation adopted and practiced differently in different organisations while in some places, the employees are required to give their suggestions only and the final decision-making authority is with the management, in other places, the workers are involved only in taking operational decisions. In some other places, workers participate in all the decisions of the organization, including those at strategic level.

The workers participation in decision making is classified into five levels. These levels are:

Informative Participation : In this participation the information regarding the balance sheet, production targets, new technology introduction etc. is shared with the workers. It is a one day communication from the management to the workers.

Consultative Participation : Here, the representatives of workers in different forms like work committees and joint management councils are consulted on various matters such as employee benefits, employee welfare and work conditions.

Associative Participation : At this level the manage-ment is under a moral obligation to accept and implement the unanimous decision of the worker's council. The role of the workers are different and more versatile in comparison to previous stages.

Administrative Participation : In administrative participation, the workers council is given certain alternatives from where it can select the one it wants to implement. The workers enjoy more here than at the previous three levels.

Decisive Participation : At this level, decisions are taken with mutual consent, so both the parties are obliged to follow each others point of views. Hence, the decisions are successfully implemented.

Worker participation in management aids two-way communication which helps the management to design and implement employee-friendly policies with minimum resistance. Since, the workers themselves participate in the decision-making process, so they cannot and do not oppose the decisions taken. With the result it boosts their morale and raises their self esteem.

Works Committees

The Industrial Disputes Act, 1949 provided to set up works committees employing 100 or more workers, comprising representatives from both the management and the workers. These committees have a president, a vice-president, a secretary and a joint secretary. The president is nominated by the employer and the vice-president and is a representative of the workers.

The basic objective to set up these works committees was to maintain harmonious industrial relations in the workplace. The duties of the committees was to sort out differences on employment related issues inbetween the management and the workers.

The works committee performs the role of consultant. It's functions include discussion of working conditions such as lighting, ventilation, sanitation etc. and amenities such as supply of drinking water, canteen facilities, medicine services, safe working conditions, administration of welfare funds, educational and recreational activities etc.

Joint Management Councils

In 1957, the Indian Labour Conference (ILC) in its 15th session, accepted the idea of setting up Joint Management Councils in India on the recommendations of Second Five-year Plan (1957-61).

Based on its recommendations, a tripartite sub-committee was constituted which came up with the idea of Joint Management Councils with basic objectives as:

- to promote cordial industrial relations
- to enhance the operational efficiency of workers
- to provide welfare facilities to workers
- to educate workers to contribute effectively to such schemes

There are some other worker participation bodies like Joint Council, Unit council, Plant council, Shop Council etc. which are similar to the Works Committee and Joint Management Council.

Another mode of worker participation in management is done through profit-sharing, gain sharing, ESOPs etc. through their involvement and share in the financial performance of the organization.

Prerequisite for Successful Participation

To make participative management successful the following conditions have to be fulfilled:

There must be free flow of information and communication between the management and the workers. This helps in removing distrust and suspicion among workers. The workers representatives must be drawn from the workers themselves since the problems and the difficulties of the workers are better understood by the workers themselves.

Strong and effective trade unionism is necessary for the success of participative management.

Workers education and training make a significant contribution to the purpose of participative management.

Neither party should feel that their position is threatened by participation.

Consultative bodies, collective bargaining and suggestion schemes make a mockery of participation management to make workers participation meaningful and purposeful.

The success of participation management depends on a suitable participative structure and attitude of both employee and employer.

The financial cost of participation should not exceed the values, economic and otherwise that come from it.

MODEL QUESTIONS

1. What do you mean by industrial relations?
2. Explain the roles of industrial relations.
3. Discuss its objectives.
4. Focus on disputes prevention machinery.
5. What is collective bargaining and what are the steps of ot?
6. Write notes on workers participation on management.

CHAPTER 13

Employee Health, Safety and Empowerment

Introduction to Safety and Health Environment

Because of the increasing complexity and hazardous nature of modern industrial operations, in 1970 the Occupational Safety and Health Act was passed. The safety and health environment manages the workplace and the whole environment of an organization to improve the productivity of both the organization and employees. So, employers and employees of any organization can be governed by Occupational, Safety and Helath Act (OSHA) formulated by both the government and the organization for the purpose of employees health and safety.

Employees need for physical and emotional security demand equal attention. By law, employers are required to provide working conditions that do not impair the safety or health of employees. Therefore, employers must provide a work environment that protects employees from physical hazards, unhealthy conditions and unsafe acts of other personnel. With the help of health and safety programmes, the physical, emotional as well as the economic security of employees may be preserved and even enhanced.

While there are laws to protect employees' physical and emotional well-being, many employers are motivated to provide desirable working conditions to human needs and rights. The more cost-oriented employers understand the value of avoiding accident and illness wherever possible. They realise that cost associated with welfare provisions like sick leave, disability retirement, replacement of injured or killed employees is exhorbitant compared to capital involved in maintaining safety and health programs. Accident and illness caused during work also affect employees' morale adversely and the organization's goodwill in the community and in the business world also gets a nosedive. Therefore, as far as possible management must create a working environment that brings about a program that facilitates employees' safety and health.

Legal Requirements for Safety and Health

In general, Occupational, Safety and Health Act extend health facilities to all employers and employees. But, there are only a few exceptions like- federal government or any state or political subdivisions of a State. Each federal agency requires to establish a safety and health programmes that are monitored by the occupational, safety and health administrative measures. Likewise, a state that desires to gain OSHA approval for the safety and health programme of its private sectors must provide similar programme that covers its state and local government employees, that is, at least as effective as its program for private employers. Where state programmes for the private sectors have been approved by the government to meet federal standard, otherwise the state carries out enforcement that would be performed by the federal government.

OSHA Standards

One of the responsibilities of the Occupational Safety and Health Administration is to develop and enforce mandatory job safety and health standards.

The OSHA standards fall into four major categories:

- general industry,
- maritime,

- construction, and
- agriculture.

These standards cover the work place, materials, equipments, machinery, power sources, protective clothing, first aid and administrative requirements.

It is the responsibility of the employers to become familiar with those standards applicable to their establishment. The federal register is the principle source of information on proposed, adapted, amended and deleted OSHA standards.

Employers Compliance with OSHA

The secretary of labour is authorized by Occupational Safety and Health Act to conduct workplace inspections, to issue citations and to impose penalty upon employers. Inspections have been delegated to the occupational Safety and Health Administration.

Work Place Inspection

A system of priorities for work place inspection has been established by OSHA as follows:

- inspection of imminent danger situations.
- investigation of catastrophes, fatalities and accident resulting in hospitalization of five or more employees.
- investigation of valid employee complaints of alleged violation of standard or unhealthful working conditions.
- special emphasis inspections are aimed at specific-hazard industries, occupations or substances those are injurious to health.
- follow-up-inspections to determine if previously cited violations have been corrected.

Creating A Safety Working Environment

The success of a safety programme mostly depends upon managers of operating departments. The human resource department coordinates the safety communications and training programs, maintains safety records required by OSHA and work closely with managers and supervisors to make the program successful.

Safety Motivation and Knowledge

Perhaps, the most important requirement of safety management for supervisors and employees is to promote safety. If managers themselves are not motivated, it would be futile to expect employees paying much attention to this vital aspect. Safety knowledge can be acquired through training. This leads to an understanding of management's policies and procedures on company safety and to fix accountabilities.

Safety Awareness Programme

Most of the organizations have a safety awareness programme that entails the use of posters, warning, safety talk and other media including pamphlets for instructing and motivating employees in the use of safe working methods. Safety awareness efforts are usually coordinated by the safety director, whose primary function is to enlist the interest and cooperation of all personnel.

Enforcement of Safety Rules

Safety rules are also emphasised in regular shop, safety meeting, new employee orientation sessions and in manuals of standard operating procedures.

Creating a Healthful Working Environment

The Occupational Safety and Health Act was designed to protect the health as well as employees. However, because of the dramatic impact of accidents, managers and employees alike may pay more attention to them than to job conditions dangerous to health. So, it is essential to identify and control the hazards. Attention should also be given to occupational illness and injuries and the impact that they have on the organization and its members. Also, health programs may be developed to provide assistance to employees suffering with health problems. Largely, as a result of a growing awareness of the general public through the efforts of environmentalists, factors in the work environment affecting health are receiving greater attention. For example, water and air pollution concerns have been drawing attention on an unprecedented scale throughout the world. This has made all of us more conscious of the immediate environment in which we live and work.

Health Hazards at Work

Unless protective measures are taken, industrial process can be a source of occupational hazards. Some of the more common health hazards are listed as—

- chemical and toxic substances such as carbon monoxide, vinyl chloride and aerosols.
- harmful dusts, smokes and fumes such as coal dust, cotton dusts asbestos.
- various types of gases, mists and vapors
- certain metals such as lead, beryllium and mercury
- radiation from *x*-rays, lasers and uranium
- infections resulted from fungi, moulds, bacterial and insects.
- extreme temperatures which may cause respiratory ailment.

EMPLOYEE EMPOWERMENT

Concept and Perspectives

Empowerment deals to make decision without approval of anyone else or absentee authority i.e. it deals with delegated authority in the area of personnel.

The necessary conditions for the empowerment of any organization are as follows:

- Participation,
- Innovation,
- Access to information, and
- Accountability.

Employee empowerment means involvement of workers in decision-making with the management. Participative managers are of the view that the workers or followers should be consulted before taking any decision or in solving the problems faced by the organisation. The result of such consultation is that groups under him work as a social unit or as a team in work performance. Employee empowerment can build good potential for team work. Participative mangers are not autocrats, nor are they free-rein mangers who abandon their responsibilities. On the other hand, they retain ultimate responsibilities for the operation of their work units. They have learned how to share operating responsibilities with those who perform the work. The result of sharing the responsibilities is that workers feel their involvement in group goals.

Employee empowerment means mental and emotional involvement of people in group activities. A person's self and not only his skill is involved. It involves a man physically as well as psychologically. Psychological involvement means an acceptance to physical involvement. Employee empowerment is not only the tables but also the ego of the person who participates. Thus, a man who participates in ego-involved instead of task involved. If the managers ask workers only for task involvement without caring for their mission. Task involvement only is not the true participation. Although, managers hold meetings, ask opinions and so on but all the time it is clear to employees that their mangers are autocratic boss. So, neither they want their ideas nor they honour their ideas. In such a case, either the employees will not support the management view psychologically or they will lose their interest in work performance as a team. Though, it keeps employees busy yet it is not a participation, because employee fails to become ego-involved.

The second underlying idea in employment empowerment is that it motivates people to contribute to the particular situation. Employee empowerment provides an opportunity to persons to take initiatives and have an idea of creativity towards the objectives of the organization. Persons take imitative in realizing the goals of the organization. In this way participation is different from mere consent. Consent means to put forth the creative ideas of mangers before the workers for their approval. They contribute nothing to the idea but simply give consent to what has been presented before tem. Employee empowerment is something more than the approval of facts already decided. It is a two-way psychological and social relationship among people rather than a procedure for imposing ideas from above.

The third idea in employee empowerment is that it encourages people to accept responsibilities in their group activities. It is a social process though which people involves themselves in group activities and wants to see the group work successfully. When people talk about their organization, they say "we" instead of "they". When organization or group feel any problem, they realize it their own problem. They become responsible citizen of the organization rather than non-responsible machine-like performers.

As the individuals begin to accept responsibilities for group activities, they begin to take interest in them and they involve themselves in getting the work done as if it is their own work and feel responsible in doing that work along with other fellow workers. They feel responsible as the team in getting the work done and it is the key step in participation. When people are interested in doing something, they will find the way to get it alone because workers think that their mangers are supportive contributors to the team: The whole group is ready to work with the manger.

In most of the cases, mangers are not willing to participate with their employees because they think that by participating with employees, they will have to share their authority and responsibility which they do not want. Because, they think that if they have responsibility why should they lose their authority? But it is not a justifiable worry because they still retain the authority. By sharing the responsibilities and authority they are losing nothing, not even the right of decision-making. It is with them. All that the manager does is make a social delegation so that the group can share in the process of decision making.

Social delegation can be compared with the formal delegation of authority in the organization. Managers like formal delegation and they do not lose their authority but it is their stock in trade and it is the act that makes them manger. Likewise in delegation where mangers lose nothing and under normal conditions they do not object to it through participation. It is their stock in trade that makes that supportive mangers.

They fear to will lose their authority by social delegation through participation. Rather, it increases their power an influence with their groups and it is a very great achievement for them because they get recognition form their group. It all creates the good human relations.

Advantages of Employee Empowerment

The advantages of employee empowerment can be summarized as below:

- It increases sense of responsibility.
- It promotes mutual understanding.
- It facilities acceptance of change.
- It improves quality of decision and employee's morale.
- It identifies capable employees.
- It provides valuable training opportunities.
- It increases overall productivity.

Disadvantages of Employee Empowerment

- It is not successful in policy matters.
- It develops confrontation between management and workers.
- Workers have a right not to participate.
- Participation is concerned with the philosophy, not followed by participants.
- Manipulation of workers by groups, individuals, cliques is possible.
- Lack of mutual trust especially in underdeveloped countries. In spite of several pitfalls, empowerment is gaining popularity among people.

MODEL QUESTIONS

1. What is OSHA?
2. Focus on its responsibilities.
3. What is employee empowerment?
4. What are the necessary conditions for the empowerment any organization?
5. What are the advantages and disadvantages of employees empowerment?

Bibliography

A. Books

Alexander, K. C.; *Participative Managements* - The Indian Experience, Shri Ram Centre for Industrial Relations, New Delhi, 1973.

Armstrong, Michale, *Handbook of Personnel Management*, Kagan Paul Ltd.; London, 1976.

Basu, K.S.; *New Dimensions in Personnel Management,* Macmillan, New Delhi, 1979.

Beach, Dale S. ; *Personnel*, Macmillan Publishing Co. New York, 1985.

Byars, Loyd R. and L.W. Rut, *Human Resource and Personnel Management*, Richard D. Irwin, Illinois, 1978.

Cox, Robert J; *Workers' Participation in Management*, International Institute of Labour Studies, Geneva, 1967.

Devis, Keith, *Human Behaviour at Work*, Tata McGraw-Hill, New Delhi, 1985.

Durbin, A.J., *Personnel and Human Resource Management*, D. Van Northland Co; New York, 1981.

Dwivedi, R.S.; *Management of Human Resources*, Oxford and IBH, New Delhi, 1980.

Employers' Federation of India, *Fringe Benefits in Indian Industry*, Bombay, 1972.

Flippo, Edwin B.; *Personnel Management*, McGraw-Hill, Kogakusha, Tokyo, 1990.

Ghosh, S.; *Trade Unionism in Underdeveloped Countries*, Bookland, Calcutta, 1966.

Civi, V.V.; *Labour Problems in Indian Industry*, Asia Publishing House, Bombay, 1972.

Halder, S.K.; *Evolution of Labour Management Relations and the Law of Industrial Disputes,* Calcutta, 1953.

Halloran, Jack, *Personnel and Human Resource Management,* Prentice Hall Inc; New Jeresy, 1986.

Indian Institute of Personal Management, *Readings in Personnel Management,* Orient Longman, New Delhi, 1970.

International Labour Organisation, *Labour Management Relations* (Report No. 23) Geneva, 1960.

Kapoor, T.N. (ed), *Personnel Management and Industrial Relations in India,* N.M. Tripathi and Sons, Bombay, 1968.

Kudchedkar, L.S.; *Aspects of Personnel Management and Industrial Relations,* McGraw-Hill, New York, 1979.

Luck, T.J.; *Personnel Administration and Appraisal,* McGraw-Hill, 1955.

Mathis, Robert L. and J.H. *Jacksan, Personnel Human Resource Management,* West Publishing Co. New York, 1982.

Miner, John B and M.G. Miner, *Personnel and Industrial Relations,* Macmillan Publishing Co.; New York, 1977.

Monappa, Arun, *Human Resource Planning and Career Planning,* IIM Ahmedabad (Mimeo).

Monappa, A.; and M.SW. Saijyidain, *Personnel Management.* Tata McGraw-Hill, New Delhi, 1993.

Myers, Charles A.; *Industrial Relations in India,* Asia Publishing House, Bombay, 1970.

Prasad, L.; *Personnel Management and Industrial Relations in Public Sector*; progressive Corporation, Bombay, 1973.

Singh, N.K. *Dimensions of Personnel Management,* Vikas Publishing House, New Delhi, 1984.

Singh, N.K. and G.K. Suri (eds), Personnel Management, Vikas Publishing House, New Delhi, 1985.

Srivastava, Suresh (ed.), *Behavioural Sciences in Management,* Asia Publishing House, Bombay, 1967.

Yoder, Dale, *Personnel Management and Industrial Relations.* Prentice-Hall of India, New Delhi, 1977.

Yoder, Dale and H.G. Heneman, *Handbook of Personnel and Industrial Relations,* Bureau of National Affairs, Washington, 1979.

B. Journals

HRD Newsletter, XLRI Jamshedpur.

Industrial and Labour Relations, Cornell University, U.S.A.

Industrial Relations, Institute of Industrial Relations, University of California, Berkley U.S.A.

Industrial Management, Industrial Management Society, Chicago, U.S.A.

Indian Journal of Psychology, New Delhi.

Indian Journal of Social Work, Tata Institute of Social Sciences, Bombay.

Indian Jornal of Training and Development, Indian Society for Training and Development, New Delhi.

C. Reports

Report of the Labour Investigation Committee, 1946.

Report of the National Commission on Labour, 1969

Report of the Bhoothalingam Committee on Wages, Incomes and Prices, 1979.

Index

D

N

O

P

❑❑❑